MW00652119

MESSAGES FROM UKRAINE

GREGG BUCKEN-KNAPP   JOONAS SILDRE

MESSAGES FROM
UKRAINE

UNIVERSITY OF TORONTO PRESS
Toronto Buffalo London

© University of Toronto Press 2022
Toronto Buffalo London
utorontopress.com

ISBN 978-1-4875-5983-0 (paper)   ISBN 978-1-4875-6151-2 (EPUB)
                                   ISBN 978-1-4875-6036-2 (PDF)

All rights reserved. The use of any part of this publication reproduced, transmitted in any form or by any means, electronic, mechanical, photocopying, recording, or otherwise, or stored in a retrieval system, without prior written consent of the publisher – or in the case of photocopying, a license from Access Copyright, the Canadian Copyright Licensing Agency – is an infringement of the copyright law.

Library and Archives Canada Cataloguing in Publication

Title: Messages from Ukraine / Gregg Bucken-Knapp and Joonas Sildre.
Names: Bucken-Knapp, Gregg, author. | Sildre, Joonas, illustrator.
Description: Series statement: EthnoGRAPHIC | Includes bibliographical references.
Identifiers: Canadiana (print) 20220398496 | Canadiana (ebook) 20220398534 |
ISBN 9781487559830 (softcover) | ISBN 9781487561512 (EPUB) | ISBN 9781487560362 (PDF)
Subjects: LCSH: Ukraine – History – Russian Invasion, 2022– – Comic books, strips, etc. |
LCSH: Civilians in war – Ukraine – Comic books, strips, etc. | LCGFT: Graphic novels.
Classification: LCC DK508.852 .B83 2022 | DDC 947.7086 – dc23

We welcome comments and suggestions regarding any aspect of our publications – please feel free to contact us at news@utorontopress.com or visit us at utorontopress.com.

Every effort has been made to contact copyright holders; in the event of an error or omission, please notify the publisher.

Proceeds from the print book will be donated to the Canada-Ukraine Foundation.

We wish to acknowledge the land on which the University of Toronto Press operates. This land is the traditional territory of the Wendat, the Anishnaabeg, the Haudenosaunee, the Métis, and the Mississaugas of the Credit First Nation.

University of Toronto Press acknowledges the financial support of the Government of Canada and the Ontario Arts Council, an agency of the Government of Ontario, for its publishing activities.

The authors acknowledge the financial support of the Swedish Institute, an agency of the Government of Sweden, for their research.

To the people of Ukraine

Contents

ON FEBRUARY 24, 2022, RUSSIA LAUNCHED
A FULL-SCALE WAR AGAINST UKRAINE.

SINCE 2018, GREGG HAS BEEN ORGANIZING AN ANNUAL
MIGRATION AND INTEGRATION TRAINING MODULE FOR YOUNG
PROFESSIONALS IN THE EASTERN PARTNERSHIP COUNTRIES
AND BALTIC SEA REGION AS PART OF THE SWEDISH INSTITUTE
ACADEMY FOR YOUNG PROFESSIONALS (SAYP) PROGRAM.

WHEN THE FULL-SCALE INVASION
TOOK PLACE, GREGG REACHED OUT
TO UKRAINIAN SAYP ALUMNI, AND TO
OTHER UKRAINIANS TAKING PART IN
ALUMNI-ORGANIZED EVENTS.

2

FEB. 24

JUST CHECKING IN TO LET YOU KNOW THAT ALL OF THE SAYP ORGANIZERS ARE THINKING OF EACH AND EVERY ONE OF THE UKRAINIAN SAYP ALUMNI.

IF YOU WIND UP NEEDING ANYTHING — TELL ME.

FEB. 26

IF YOU WOULD LIKE TO COME TO SWEDEN, THE SAYP ORGANIZERS HERE HAVE BEEN WORKING ON A PLAN TO SECURE SHORT-TERM HOUSING (FREE OF COURSE) FOR OUR UKRAINIAN ALUMNI. IT WOULD LIKELY BE A FEW DAYS OR A WEEK AT A TIME AT ONE PERSON'S PLACE, AND THEN ON TO SOMEWHERE ELSE IN THE SAME CITY. BUT IT WOULD BE SAFE AND FREE, AND WE WOULD BE HAPPY TO TRY TO FIND YOU THAT TYPE OF POSSIBILITY HERE.

SO: IF YOU ARE INTERESTED IN COMING TO SWEDEN, LET ME KNOW.

STAY SAFE!

HERE ARE SOME OF THE RESPONSES THAT HE RECEIVED.

AND THE IMAGES THAT CAME TO MIND WHILE HE READ THE MESSAGES.

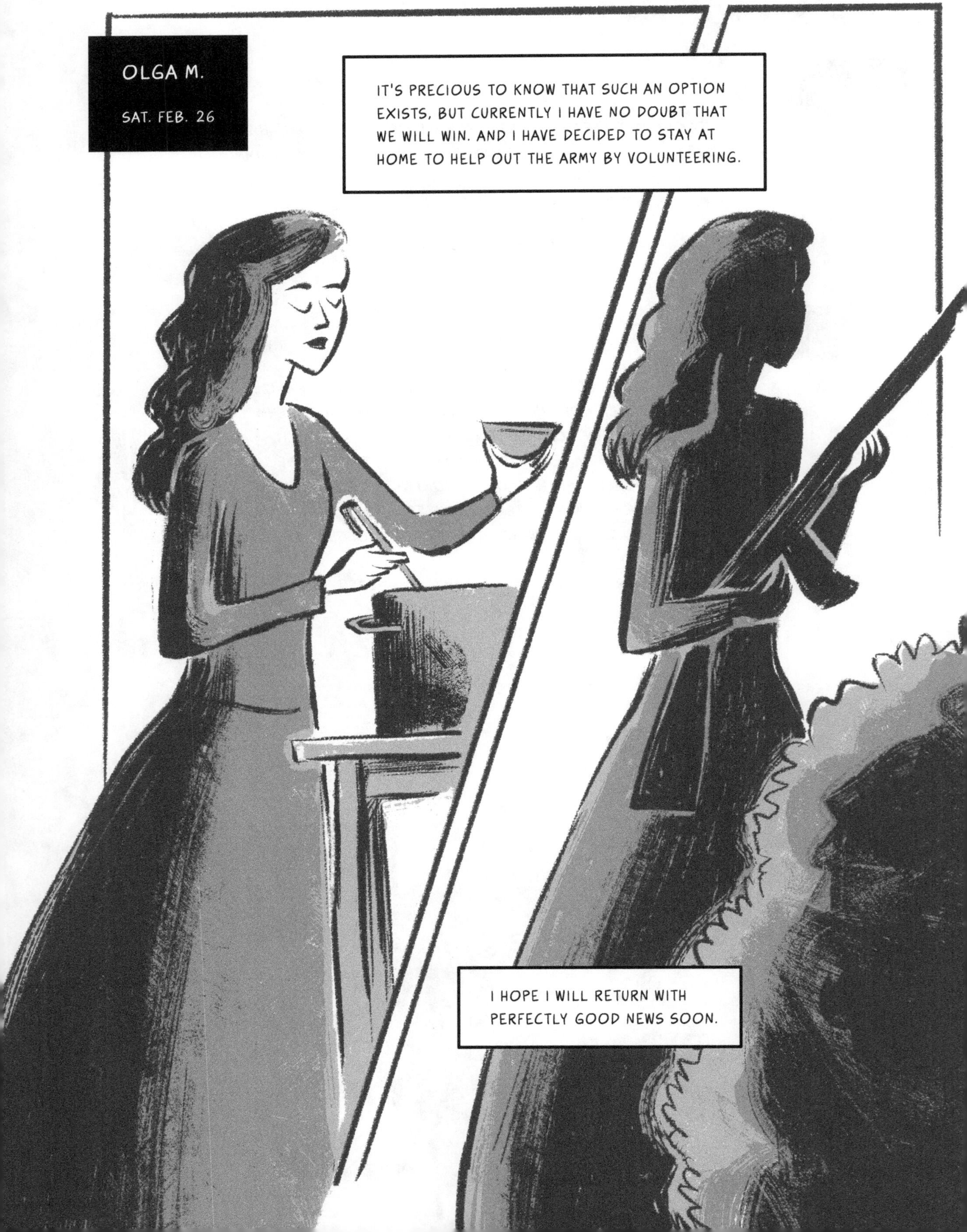
OLGA M.
SAT. FEB. 26
IT'S PRECIOUS TO KNOW THAT SUCH AN OPTION EXISTS, BUT CURRENTLY I HAVE NO DOUBT THAT WE WILL WIN. AND I HAVE DECIDED TO STAY AT HOME TO HELP OUT THE ARMY BY VOLUNTEERING.
I HOPE I WILL RETURN WITH PERFECTLY GOOD NEWS SOON.

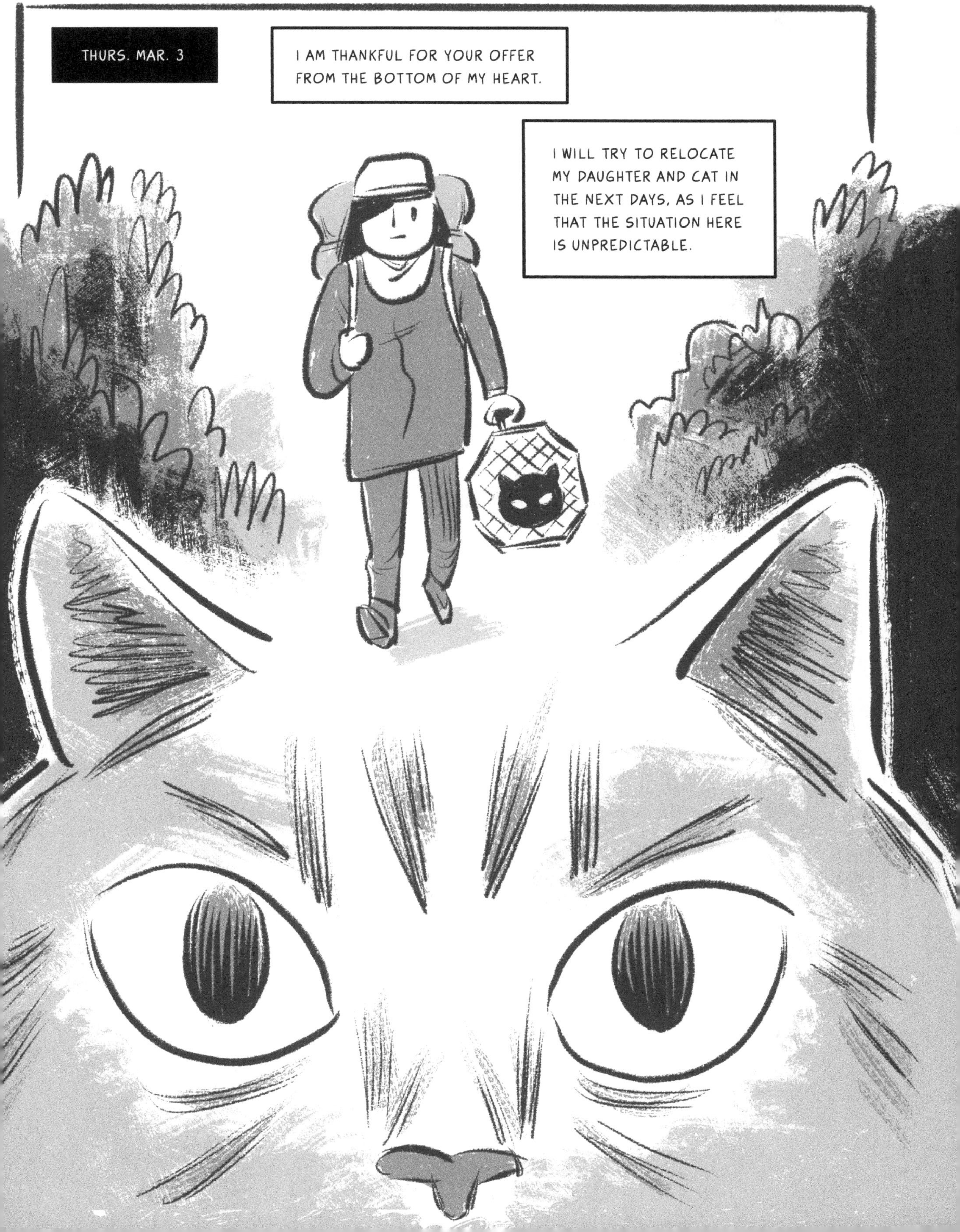
THURS. MAR. 3
I AM THANKFUL FOR YOUR OFFER FROM THE BOTTOM OF MY HEART.
I WILL TRY TO RELOCATE MY DAUGHTER AND CAT IN THE NEXT DAYS, AS I FEEL THAT THE SITUATION HERE IS UNPREDICTABLE.

OLGA I.
SAT. FEB. 26
THANKS A LOT, I WILL THINK ABOUT IT.
BUT SO FAR I CAN'T EVEN LEAVE MY DISTRICT AS WE HAVE A CURFEW AND ALSO ALL THE BRIDGES ARE BLOCKED (AND WILL BE BLASTED IF THE ENEMY GETS TOO CLOSE).
ANYWAY, I TRY TO BE SAFE, AND I HAVE ALL THAT IS NECESSARY.

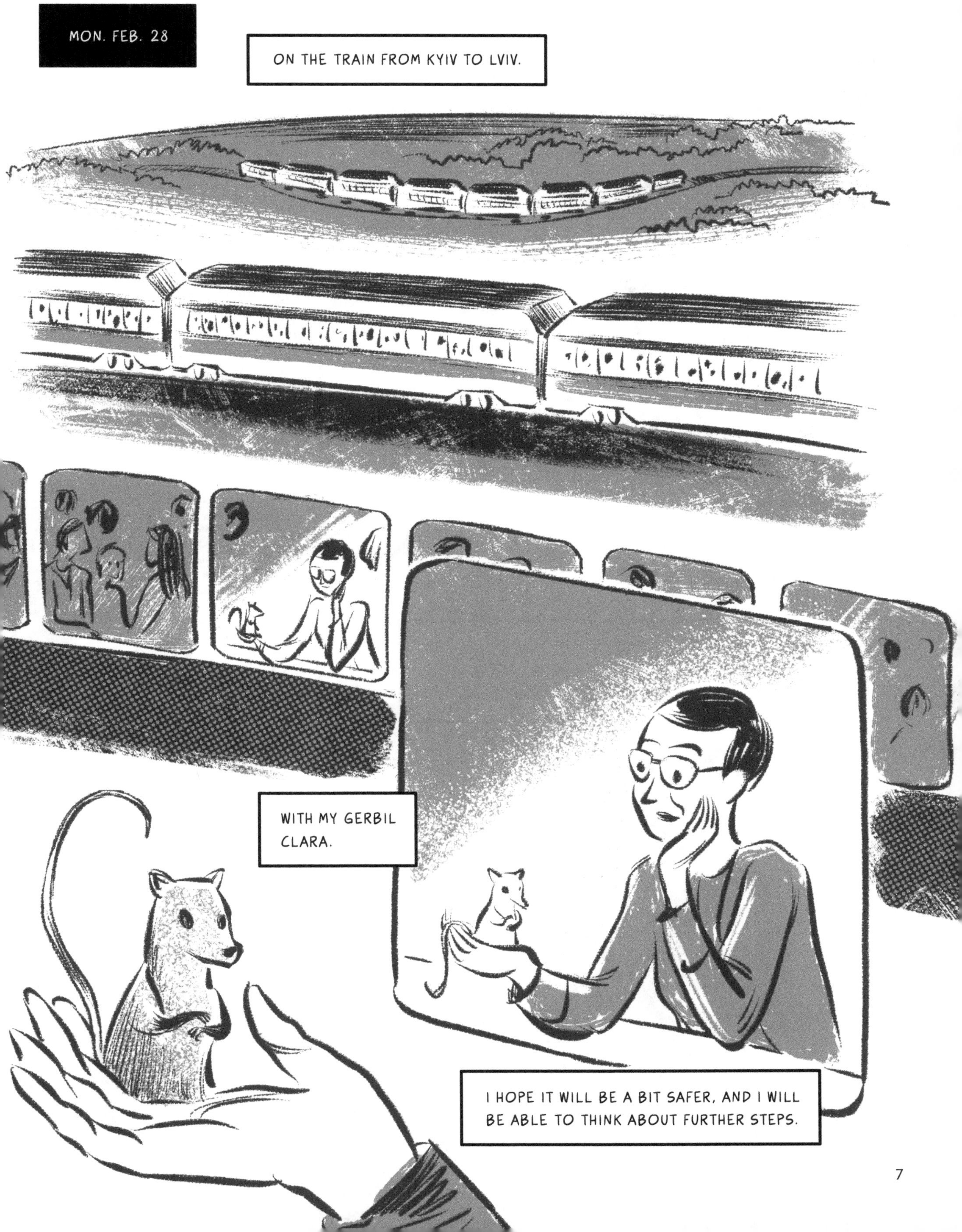

MON. FEB. 28
ON THE TRAIN FROM KYIV TO LVIV.
WITH MY GERBIL CLARA.
I HOPE IT WILL BE A BIT SAFER, AND I WILL BE ABLE TO THINK ABOUT FURTHER STEPS.

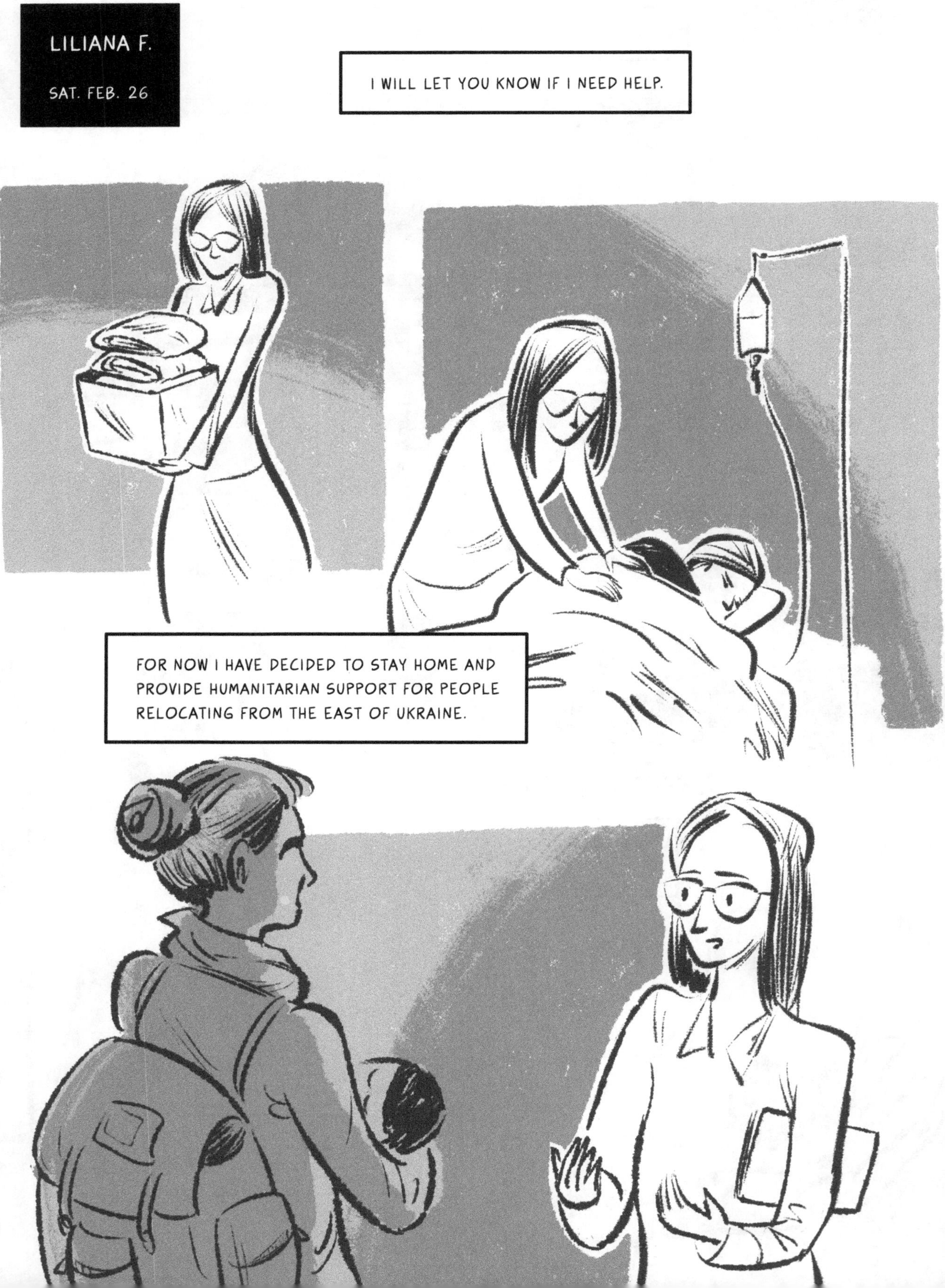
LILIANA F.
SAT. FEB. 26
I WILL LET YOU KNOW IF I NEED HELP.
FOR NOW I HAVE DECIDED TO STAY HOME AND PROVIDE HUMANITARIAN SUPPORT FOR PEOPLE RELOCATING FROM THE EAST OF UKRAINE.

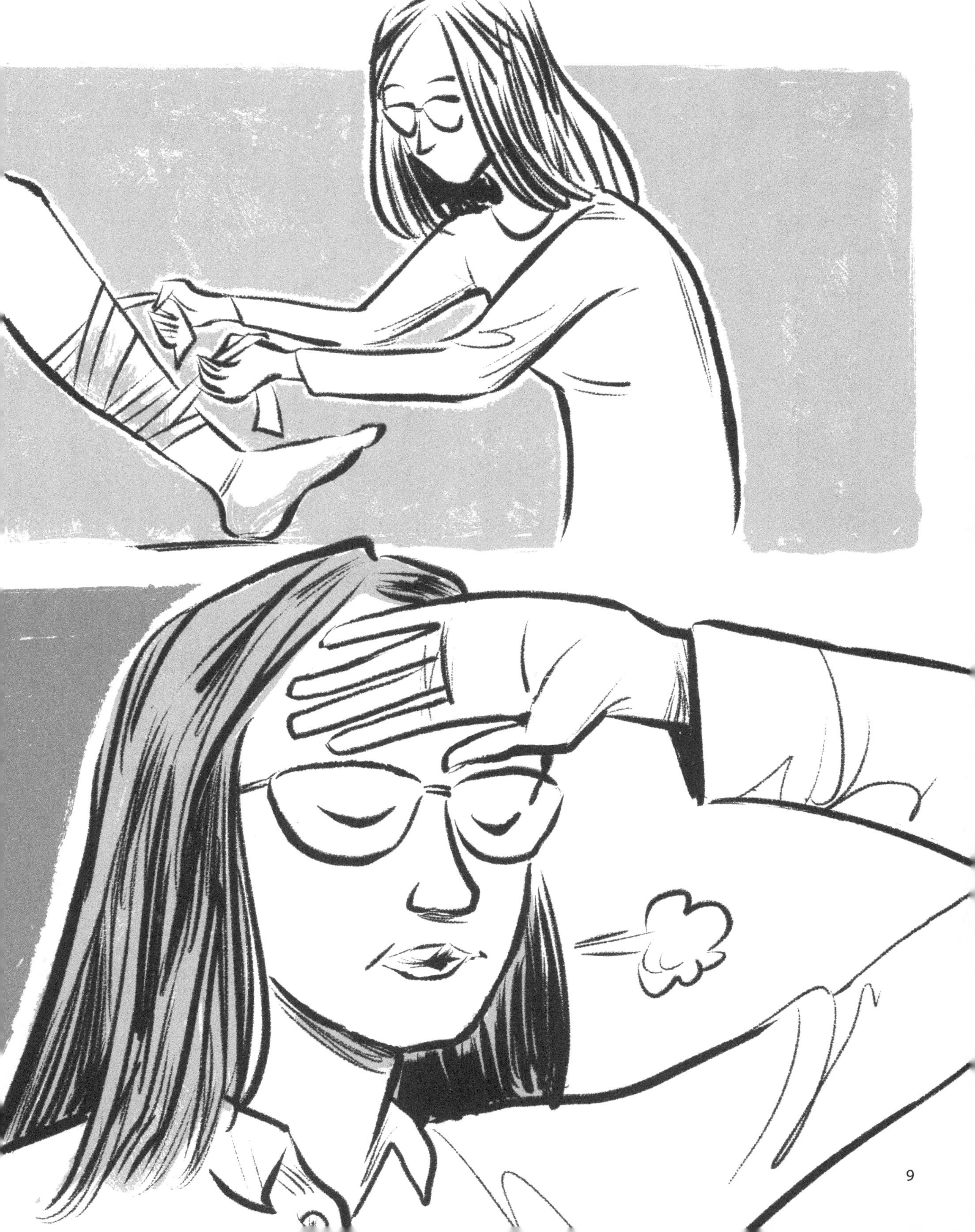

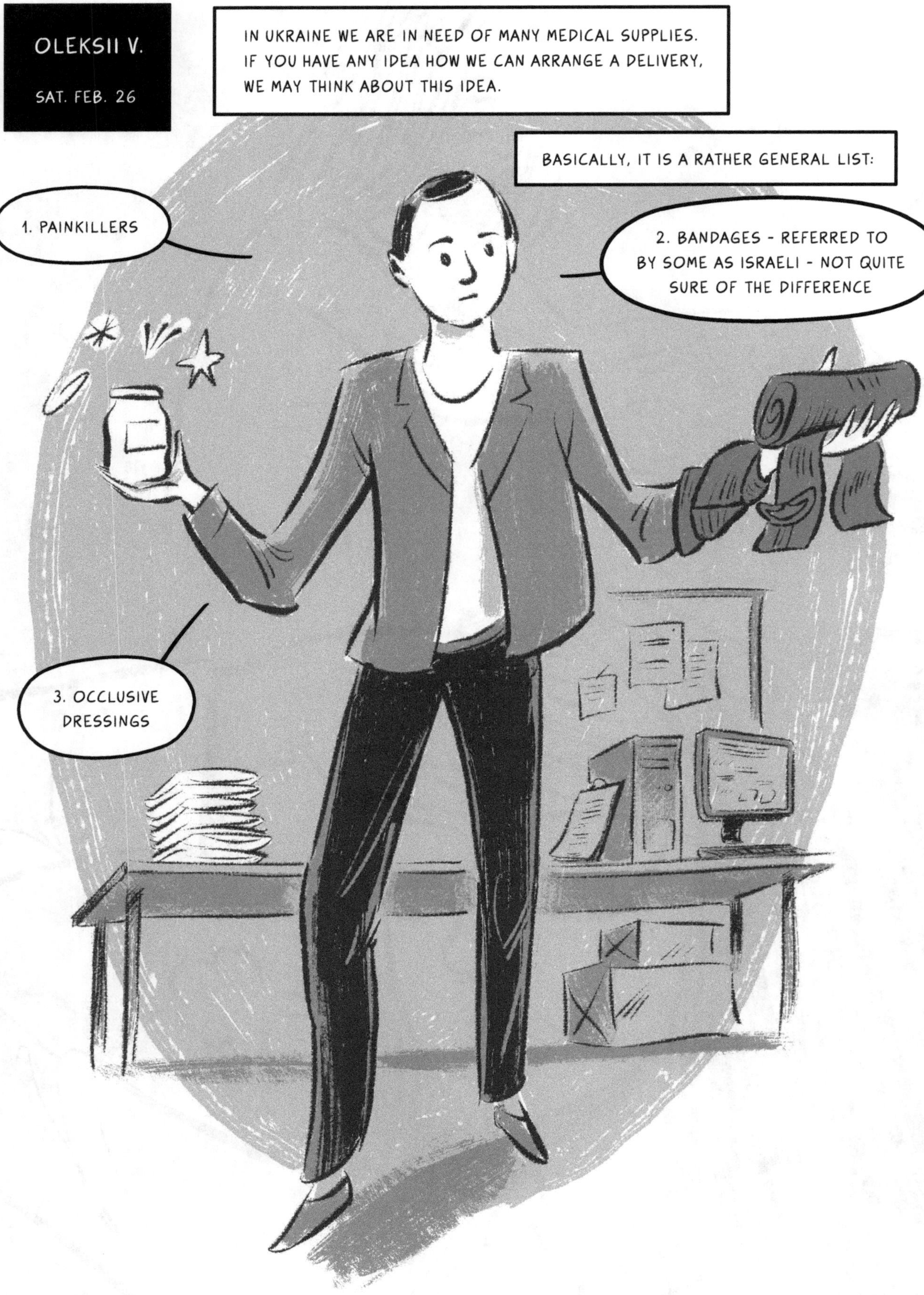
OLEKSII V.
SAT. FEB. 26
IN UKRAINE WE ARE IN NEED OF MANY MEDICAL SUPPLIES. IF YOU HAVE ANY IDEA HOW WE CAN ARRANGE A DELIVERY, WE MAY THINK ABOUT THIS IDEA.
BASICALLY, IT IS A RATHER GENERAL LIST:
1. PAINKILLERS
2. BANDAGES - REFERRED TO BY SOME AS ISRAELI - NOT QUITE SURE OF THE DIFFERENCE
3. OCCLUSIVE DRESSINGS

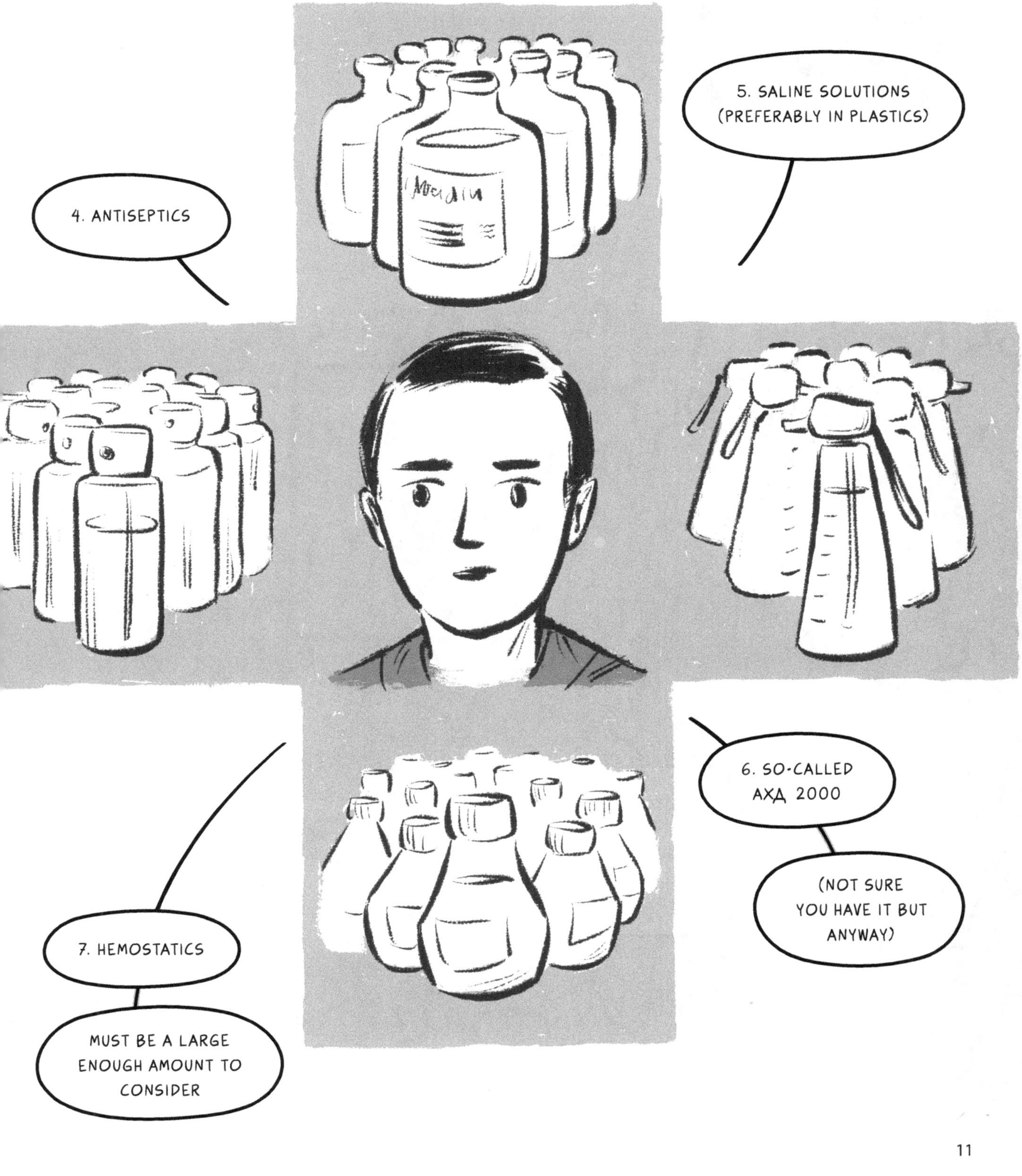
4. ANTISEPTICS
5. SALINE SOLUTIONS (PREFERABLY IN PLASTICS)
6. SO-CALLED АХД 2000
(NOT SURE YOU HAVE IT BUT ANYWAY)
7. HEMOSTATICS
MUST BE A LARGE ENOUGH AMOUNT TO CONSIDER

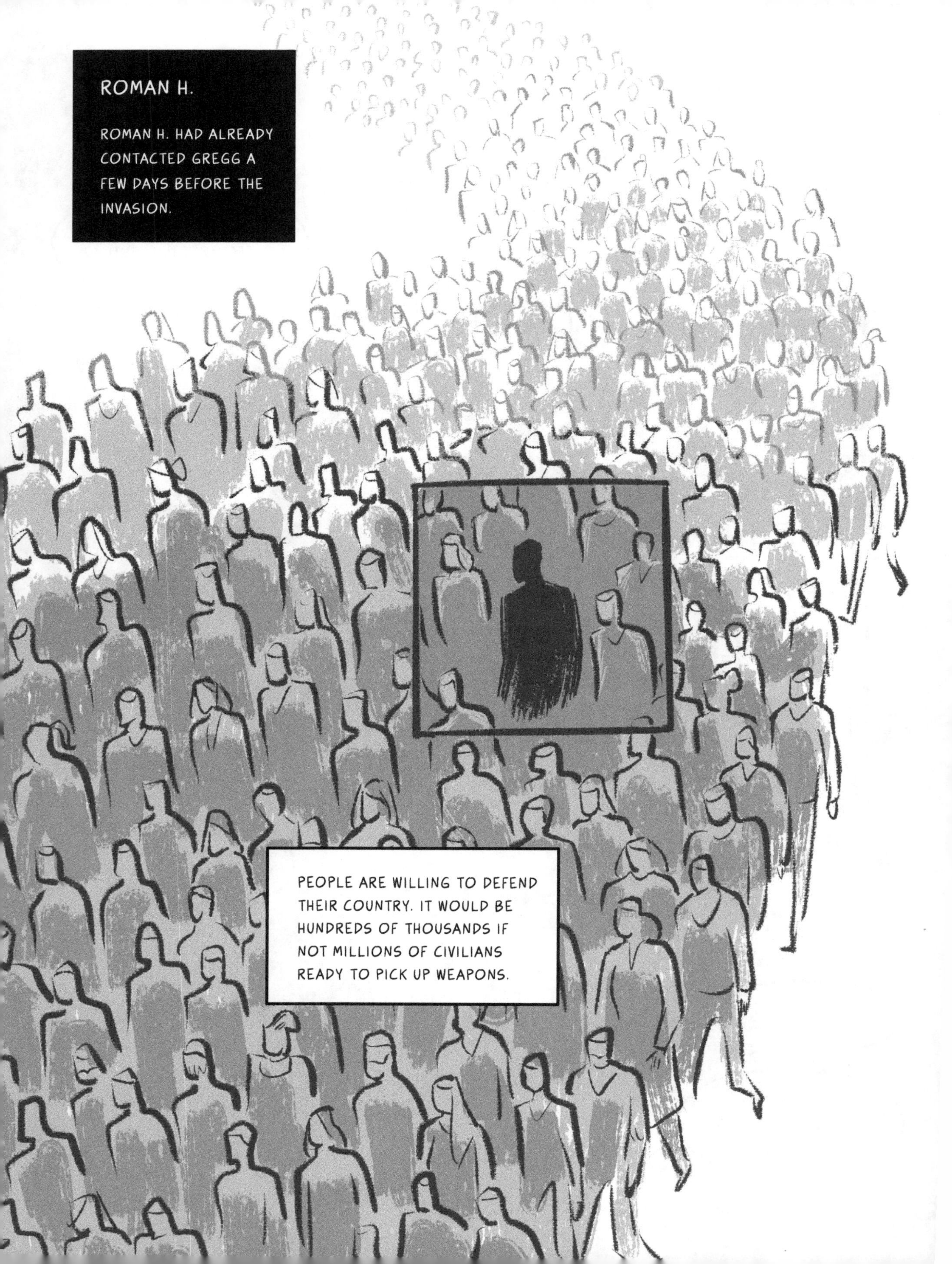
ROMAN H.
ROMAN H. HAD ALREADY CONTACTED GREGG A FEW DAYS BEFORE THE INVASION.
PEOPLE ARE WILLING TO DEFEND THEIR COUNTRY. IT WOULD BE HUNDREDS OF THOUSANDS IF NOT MILLIONS OF CIVILIANS READY TO PICK UP WEAPONS.

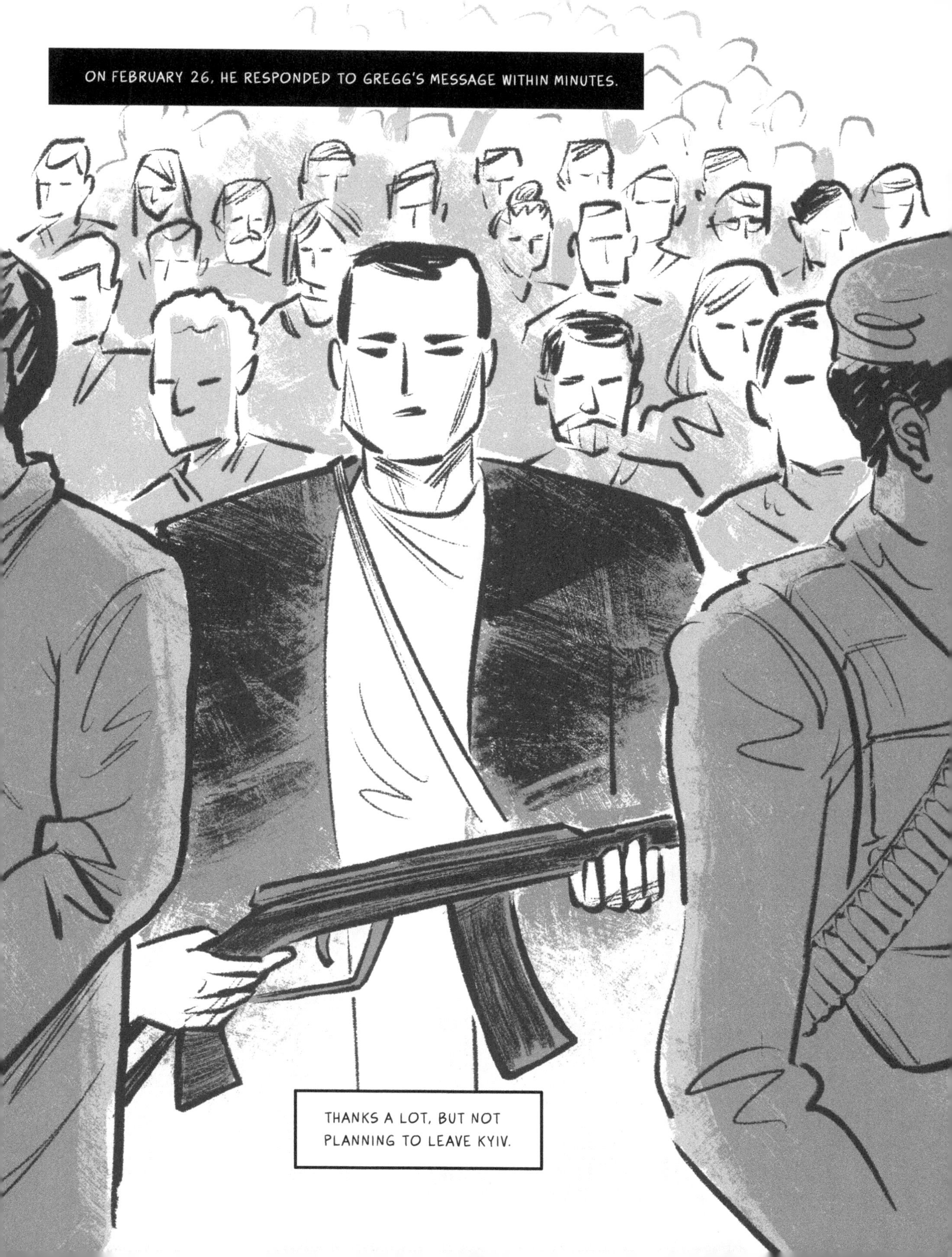
ON FEBRUARY 26, HE RESPONDED TO GREGG'S MESSAGE WITHIN MINUTES.
THANKS A LOT, BUT NOT PLANNING TO LEAVE KYIV.

TAISIIA D.

FRI. FEB. 25

I AM IN THE METRO MOVING TO THE OUTSKIRTS OF THE CITY. FEELING TOO SCARED TO STAY AT MY HOUSE, WHICH IS TO THE NORTH TOWARD CHERNOBYL.

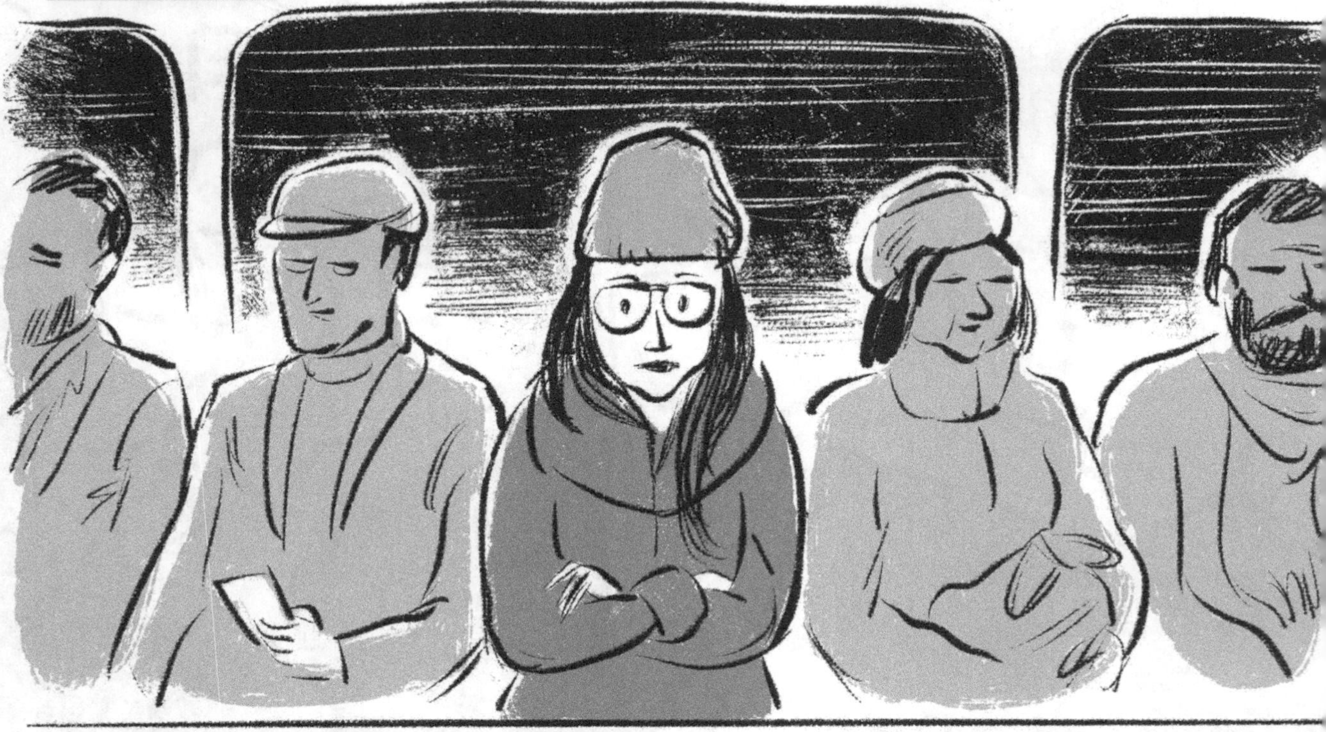

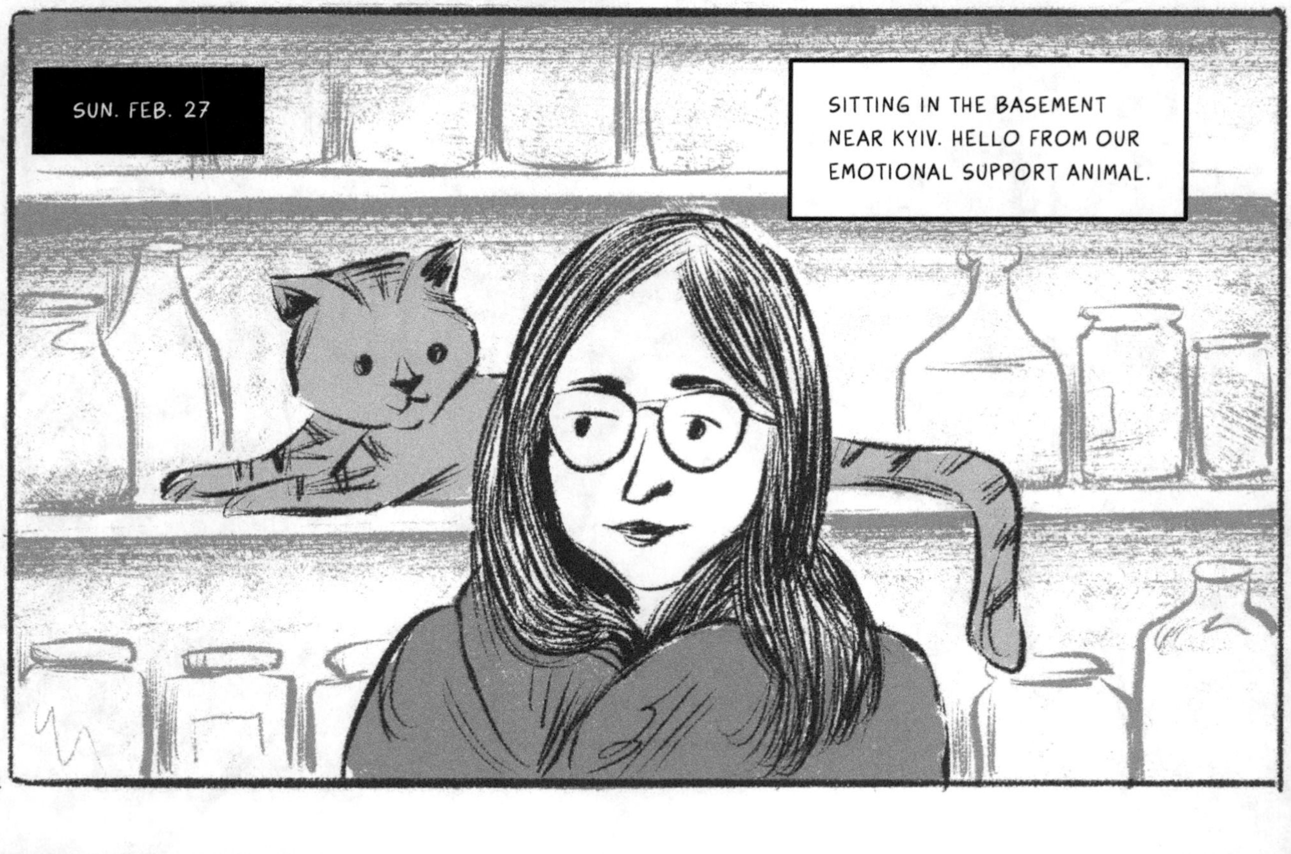
SUN. FEB. 27
SITTING IN THE BASEMENT NEAR KYIV. HELLO FROM OUR EMOTIONAL SUPPORT ANIMAL.

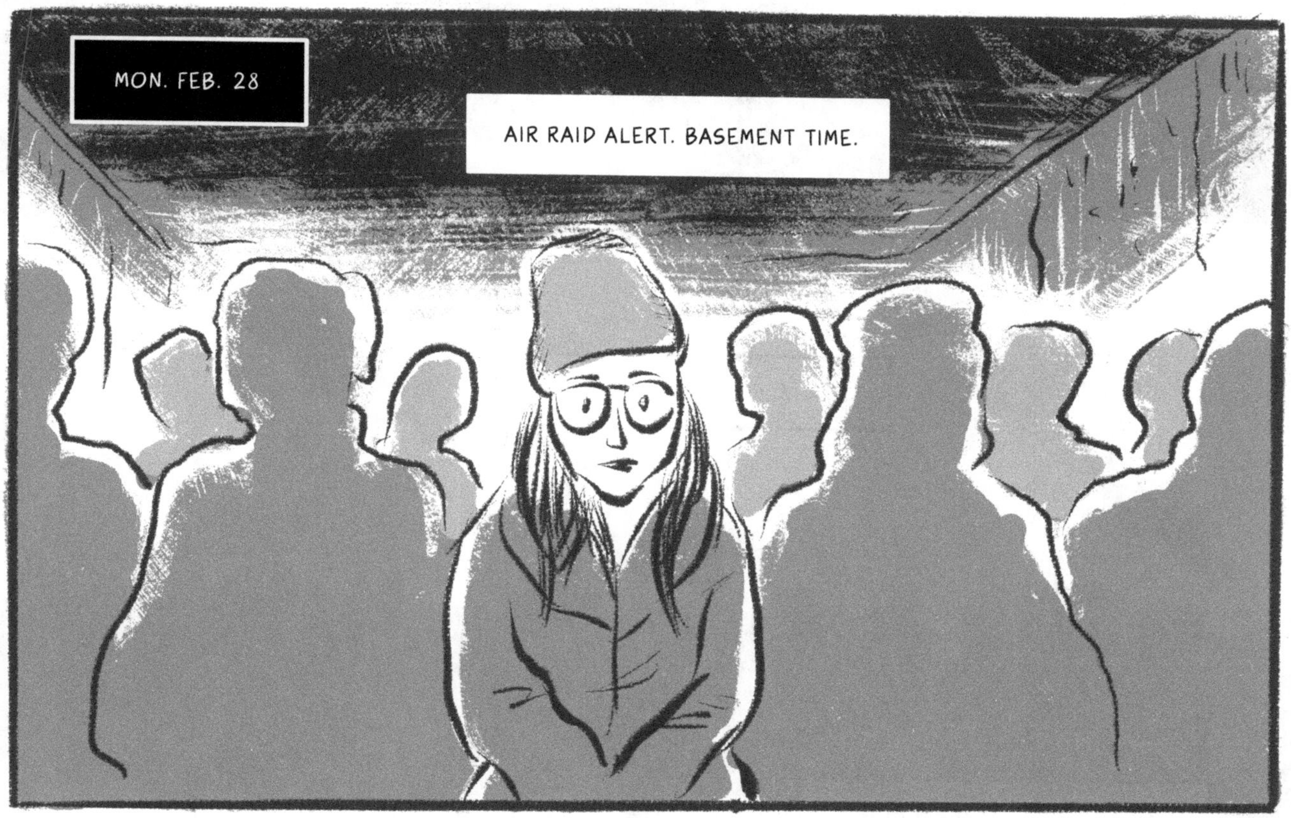
MON. FEB. 28
AIR RAID ALERT. BASEMENT TIME.

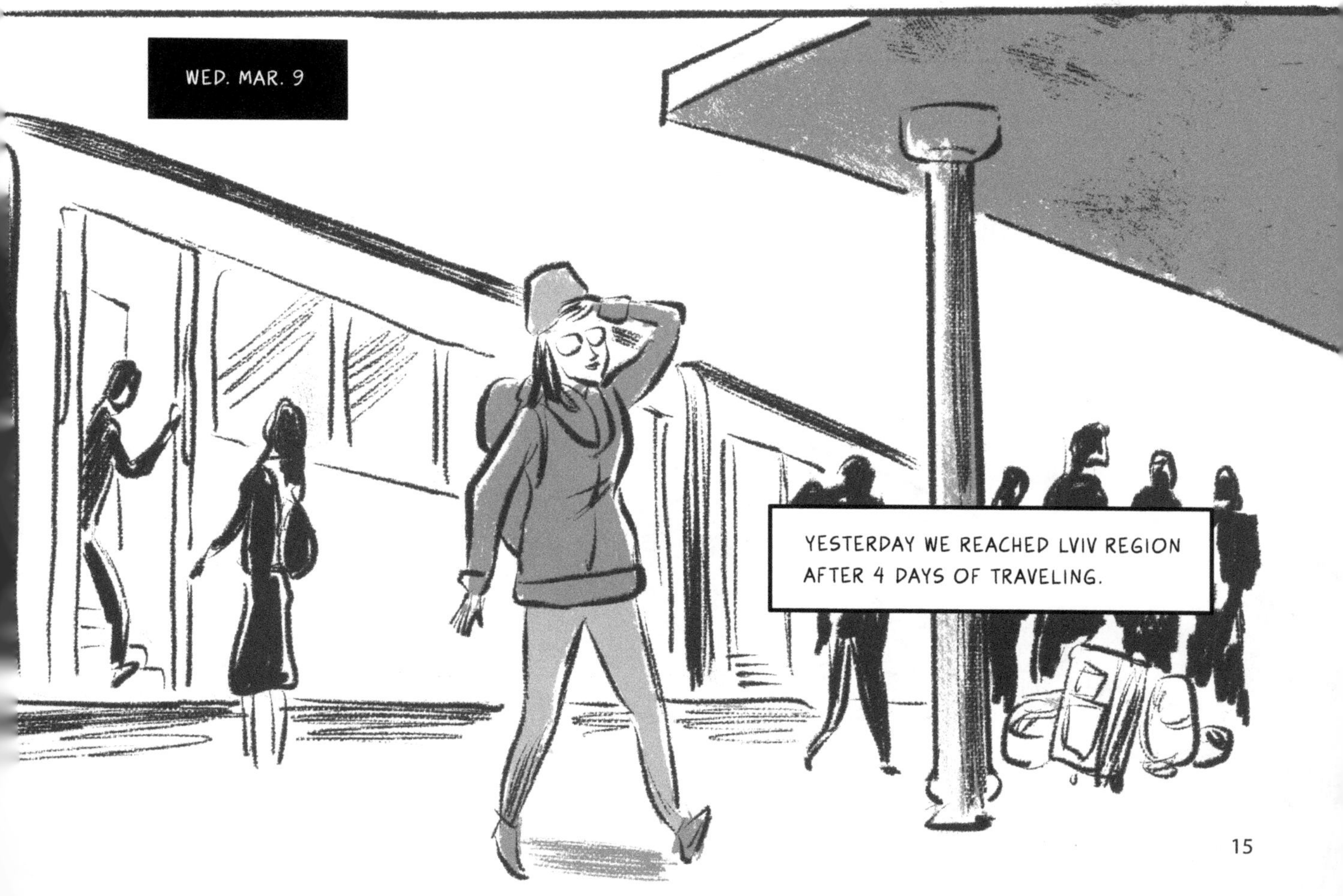
WED. MAR. 9
YESTERDAY WE REACHED LVIV REGION AFTER 4 DAYS OF TRAVELING.

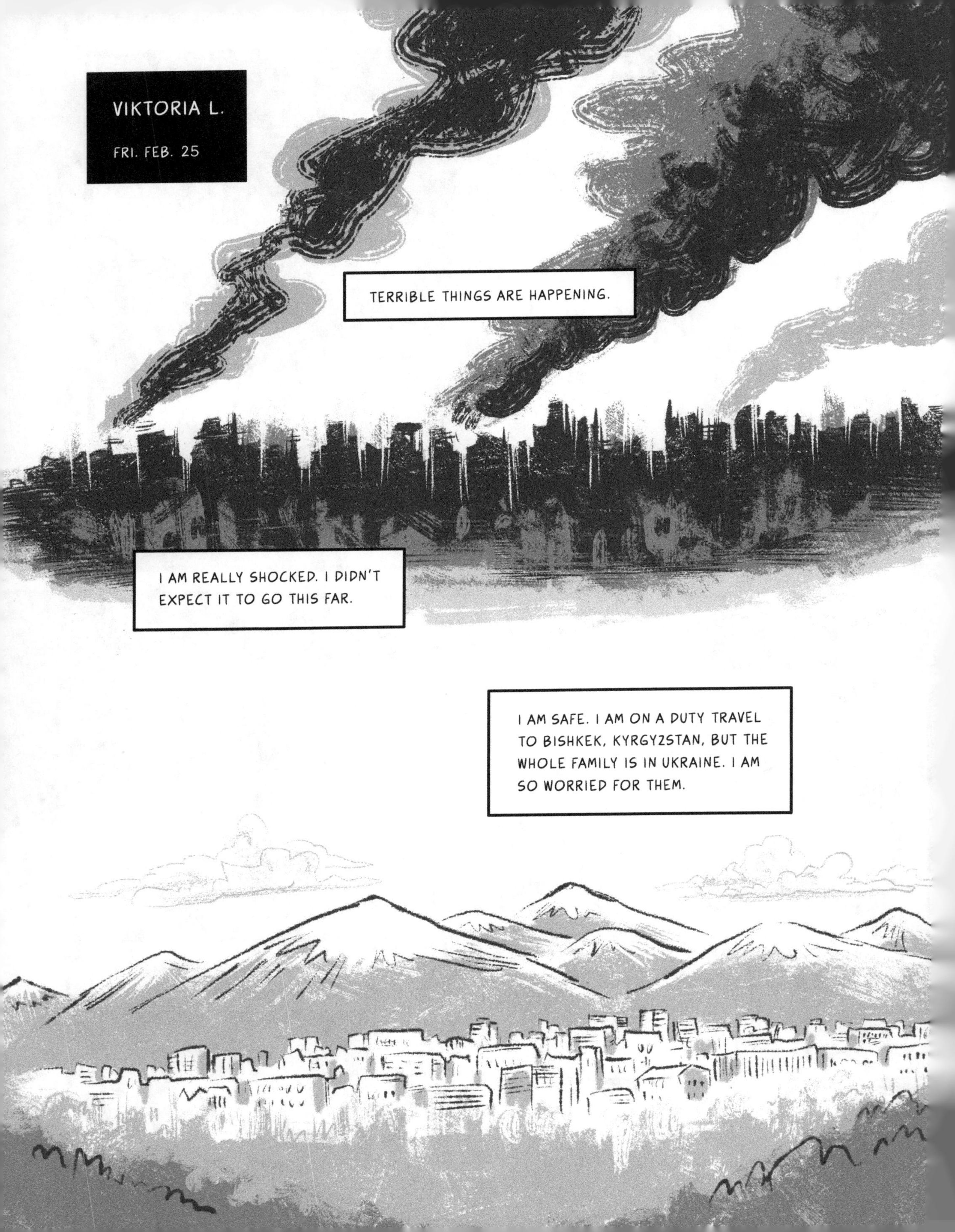

VIKTORIA L.
FRI. FEB. 25
TERRIBLE THINGS ARE HAPPENING.
I AM REALLY SHOCKED. I DIDN'T EXPECT IT TO GO THIS FAR.
I AM SAFE. I AM ON A DUTY TRAVEL TO BISHKEK, KYRGYZSTAN, BUT THE WHOLE FAMILY IS IN UKRAINE. I AM SO WORRIED FOR THEM.

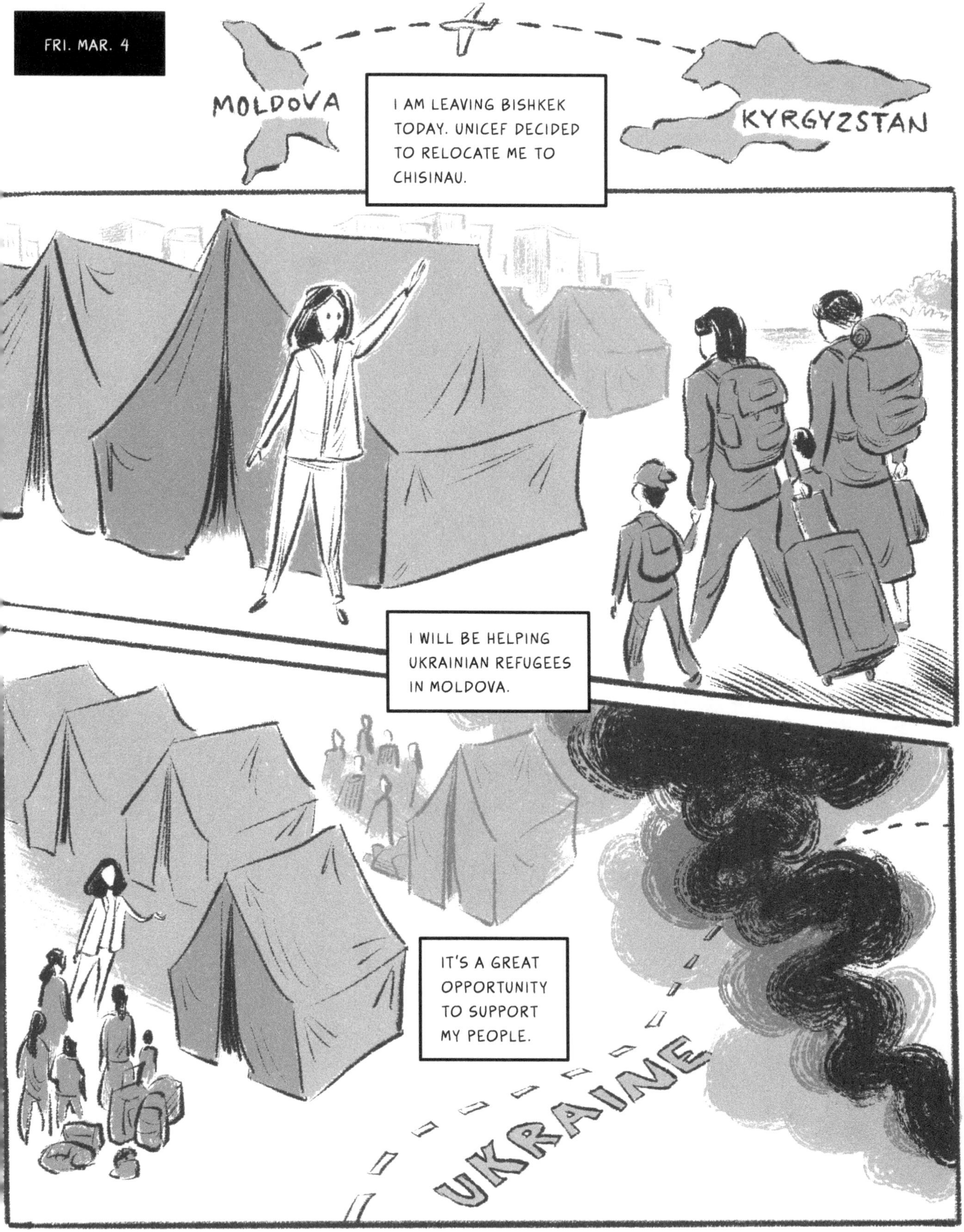
FRI. MAR. 4
MOLDOVA
I AM LEAVING BISHKEK TODAY. UNICEF DECIDED TO RELOCATE ME TO CHISINAU.
KYRGYZSTAN
I WILL BE HELPING UKRAINIAN REFUGEES IN MOLDOVA.
IT'S A GREAT OPPORTUNITY TO SUPPORT MY PEOPLE.
UKRAINE

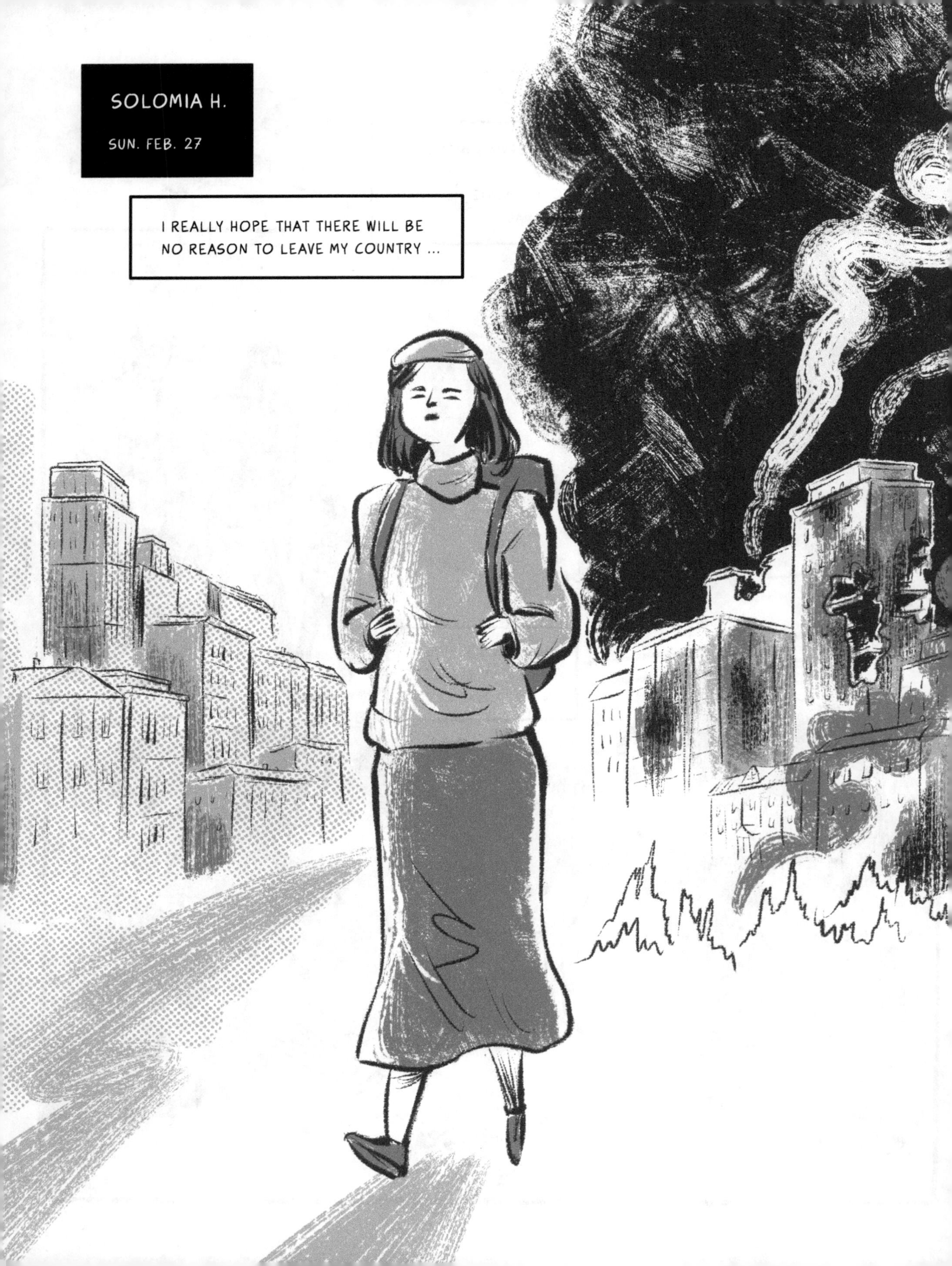
SOLOMIA H.
SUN. FEB. 27
I REALLY HOPE THAT THERE WILL BE NO REASON TO LEAVE MY COUNTRY ...

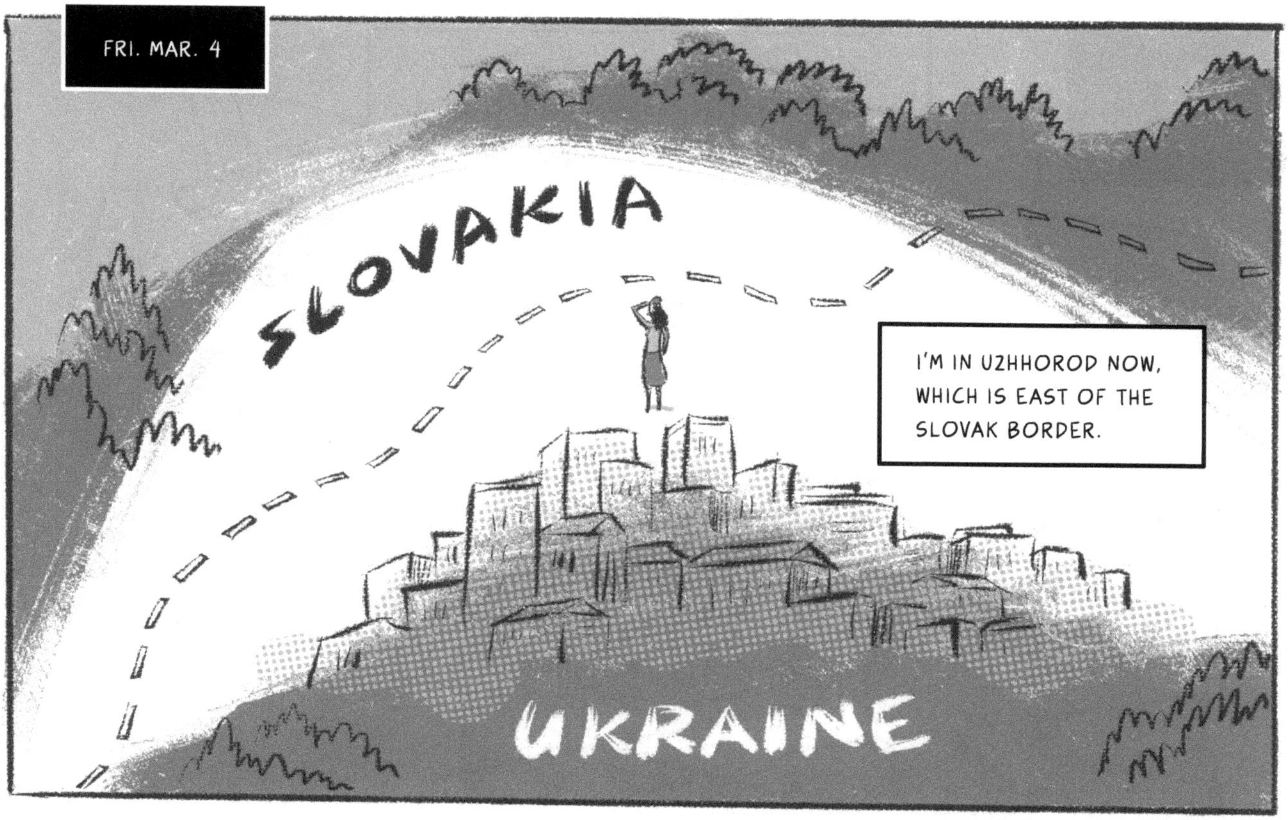
FRI. MAR. 4
SLOVAKIA
I'M IN UZHHOROD NOW, WHICH IS EAST OF THE SLOVAK BORDER.
UKRAINE

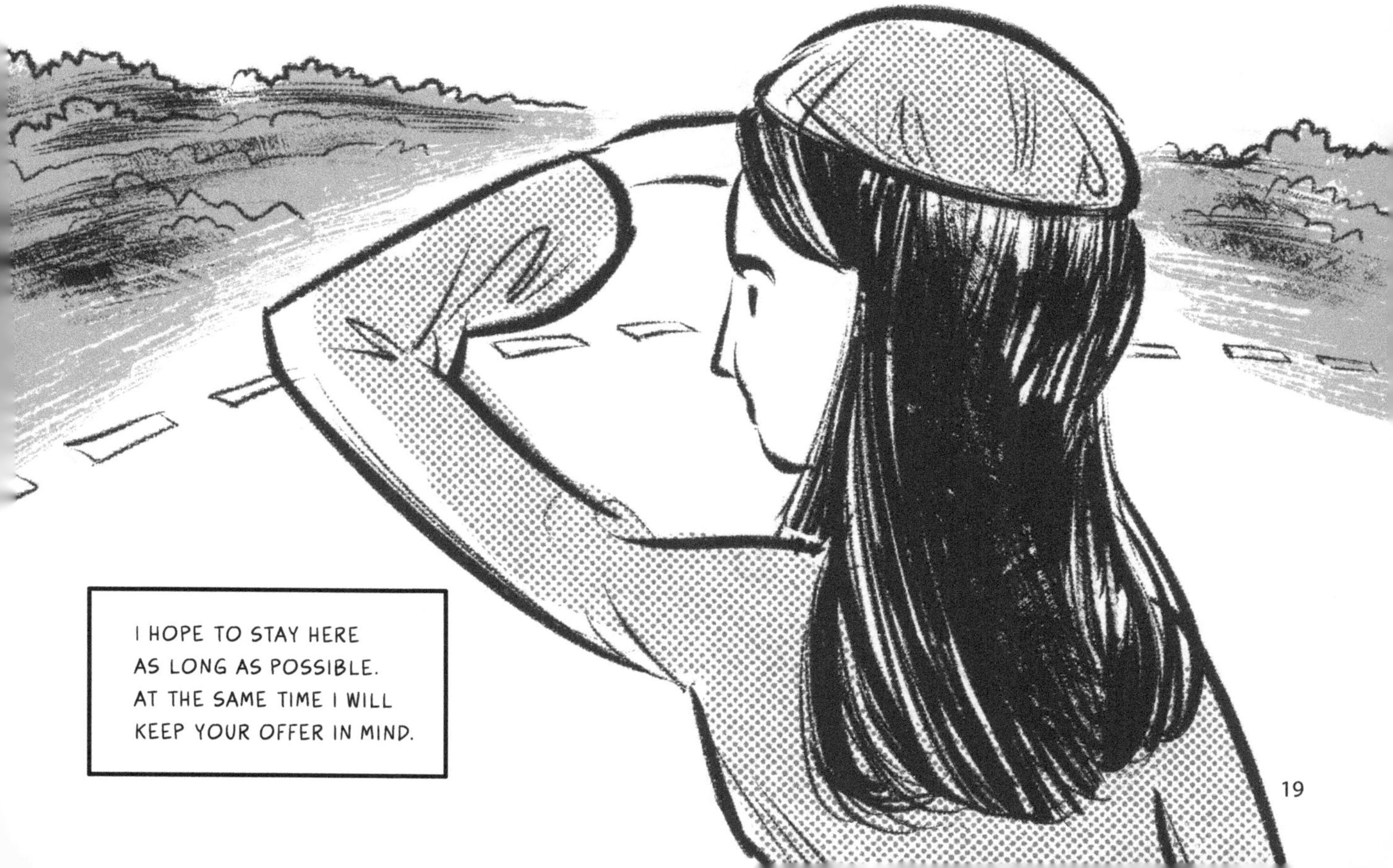
I HOPE TO STAY HERE AS LONG AS POSSIBLE. AT THE SAME TIME I WILL KEEP YOUR OFFER IN MIND.

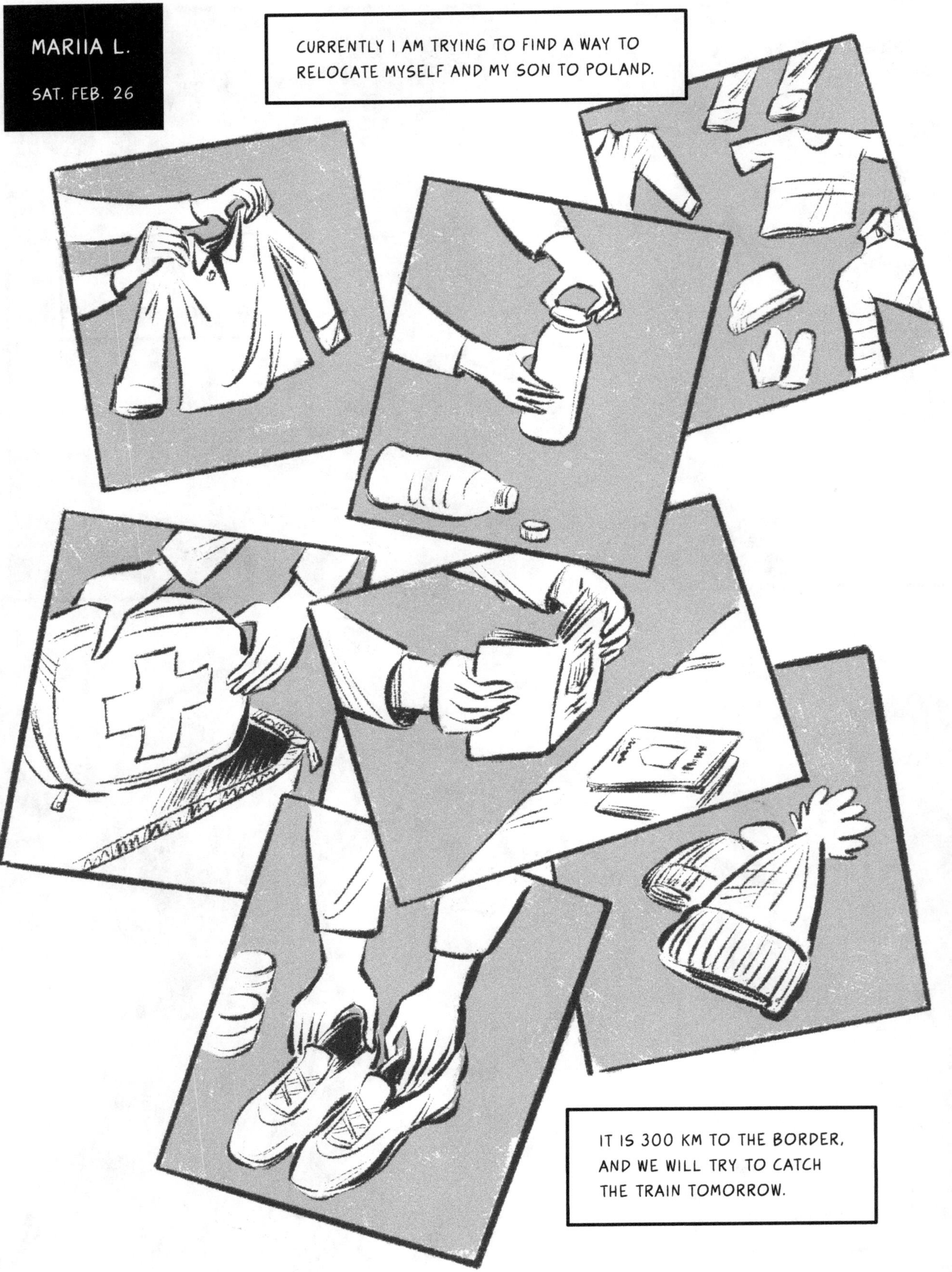
MARIIA L.
SAT. FEB. 26
CURRENTLY I AM TRYING TO FIND A WAY TO RELOCATE MYSELF AND MY SON TO POLAND.
IT IS 300 KM TO THE BORDER, AND WE WILL TRY TO CATCH THE TRAIN TOMORROW.

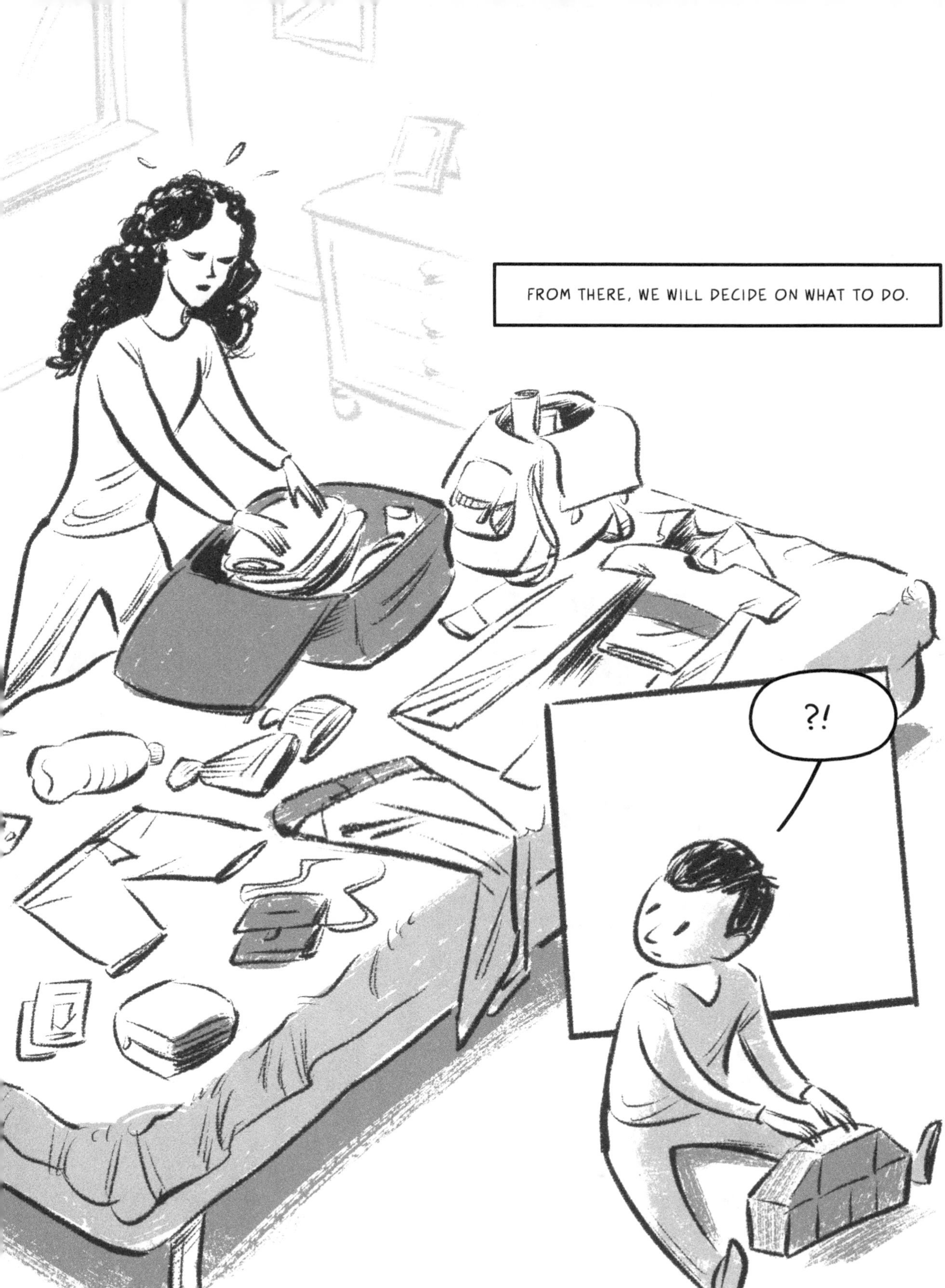

FROM THERE, WE WILL DECIDE ON WHAT TO DO.
?!

KATERINA P.
THURS. FEB. 24
MY TOWN IS ONLY 15 KM FROM KYIV, SO WE ARE HIDING AS WELL.

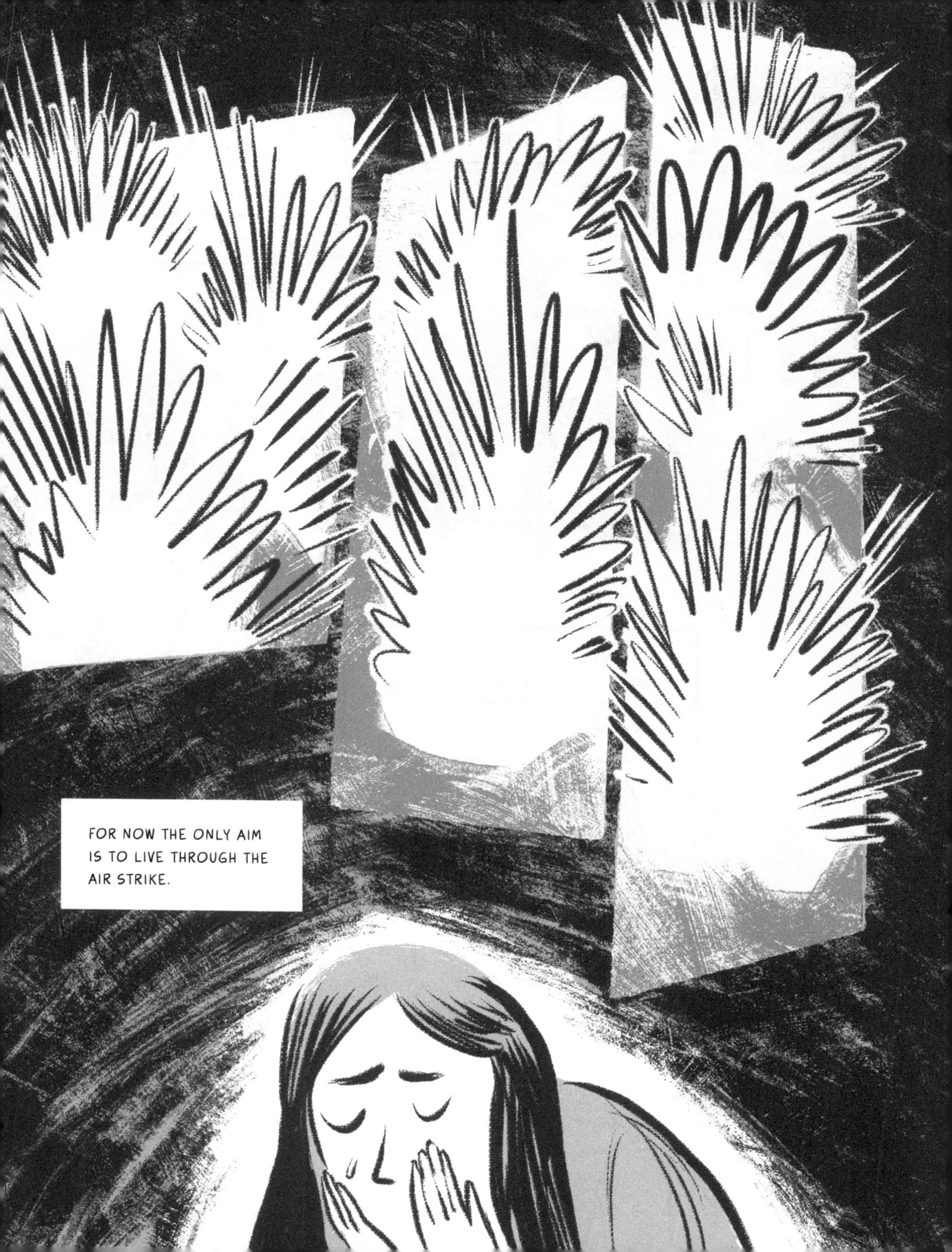
FOR NOW THE ONLY AIM IS TO LIVE THROUGH THE AIR STRIKE.

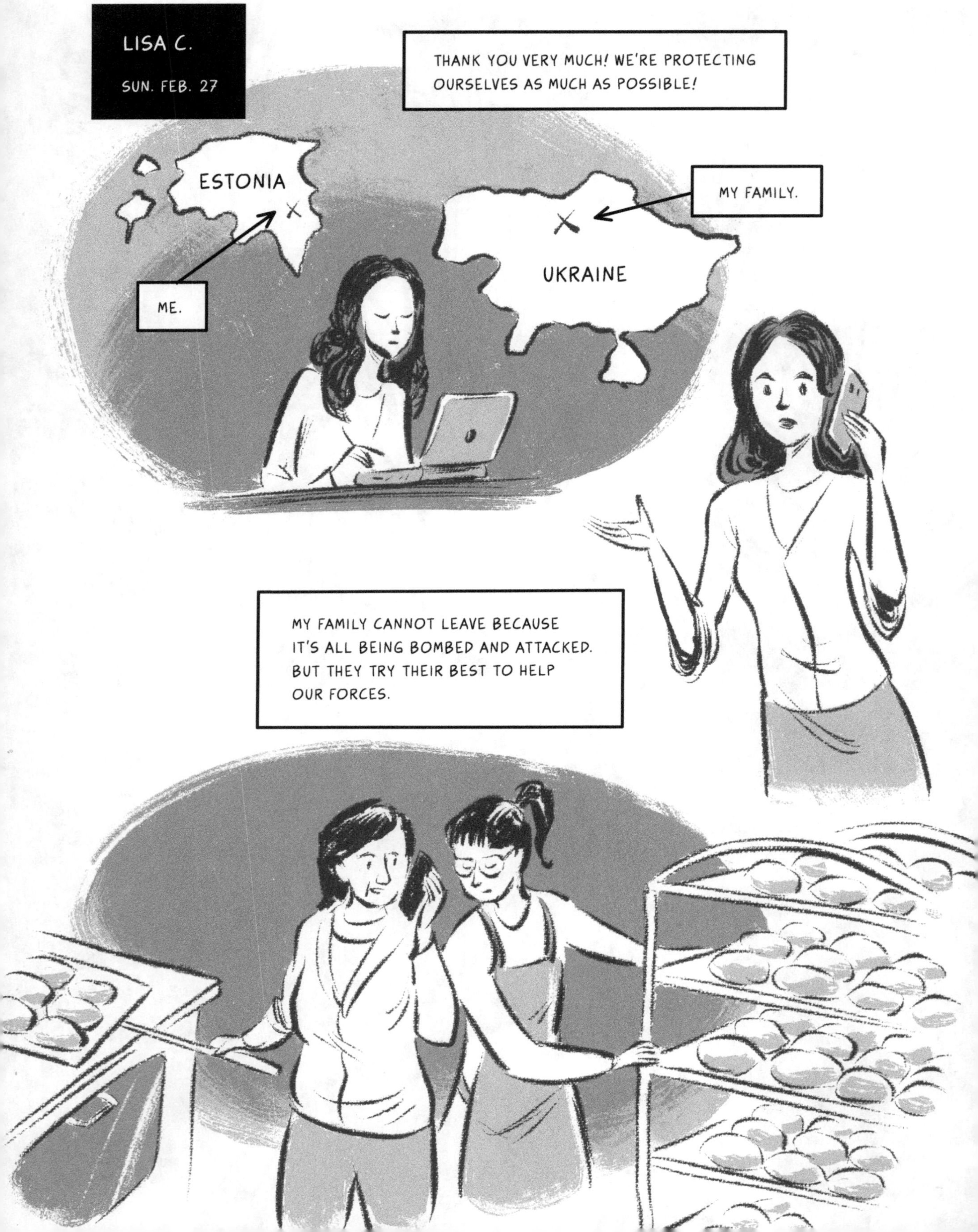
LISA C.
SUN. FEB. 27
THANK YOU VERY MUCH! WE'RE PROTECTING OURSELVES AS MUCH AS POSSIBLE!
ESTONIA
ME.
UKRAINE
MY FAMILY.
MY FAMILY CANNOT LEAVE BECAUSE IT'S ALL BEING BOMBED AND ATTACKED. BUT THEY TRY THEIR BEST TO HELP OUR FORCES.

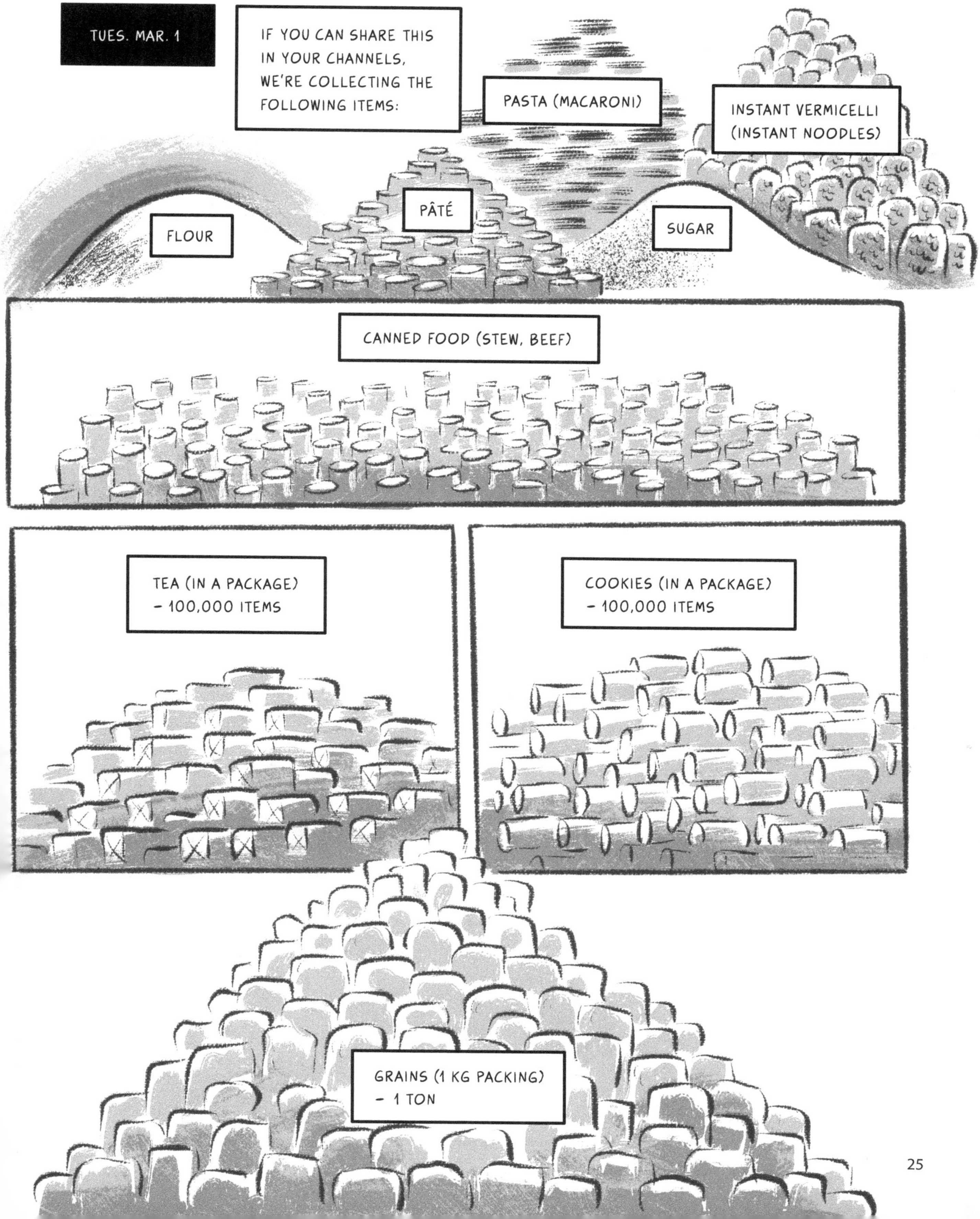
TUES. MAR. 1
IF YOU CAN SHARE THIS IN YOUR CHANNELS, WE'RE COLLECTING THE FOLLOWING ITEMS:
PASTA (MACARONI)
INSTANT VERMICELLI (INSTANT NOODLES)
FLOUR
PÂTÉ
SUGAR
CANNED FOOD (STEW, BEEF)
TEA (IN A PACKAGE) – 100,000 ITEMS
COOKIES (IN A PACKAGE) – 100,000 ITEMS
GRAINS (1 KG PACKING) – 1 TON

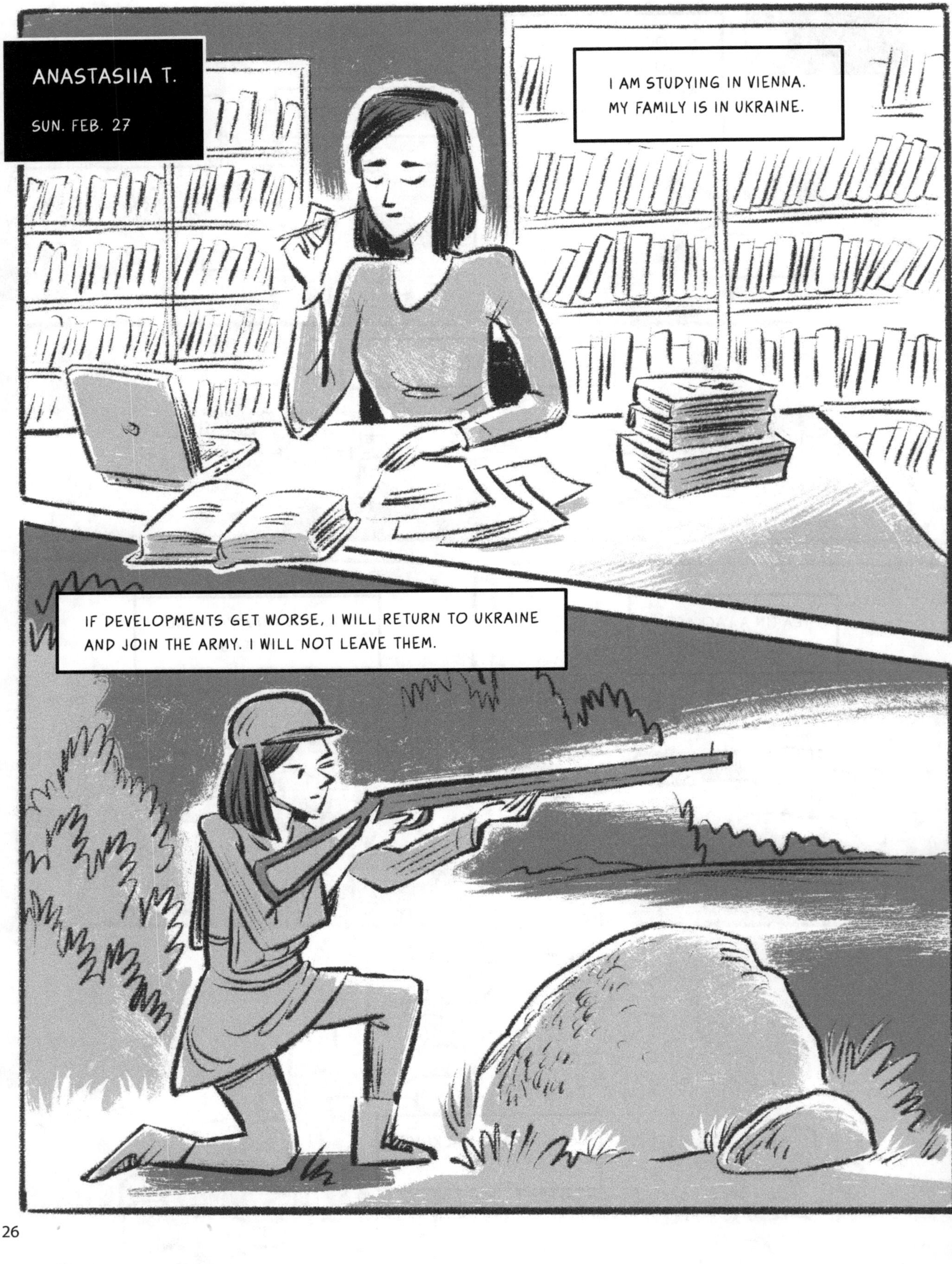
ANASTASIIA T.
SUN. FEB. 27
I AM STUDYING IN VIENNA. MY FAMILY IS IN UKRAINE.
IF DEVELOPMENTS GET WORSE, I WILL RETURN TO UKRAINE AND JOIN THE ARMY. I WILL NOT LEAVE THEM.

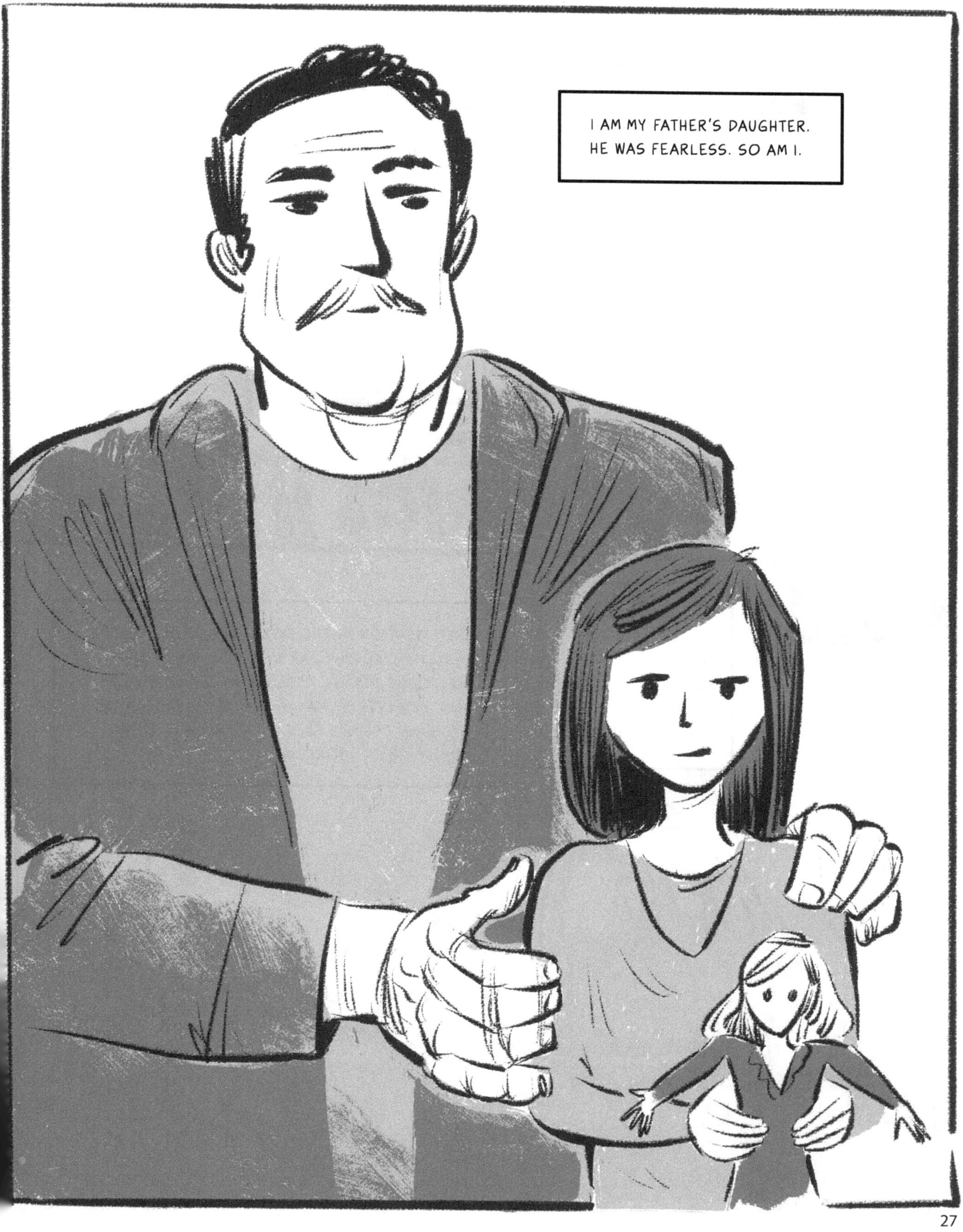
I AM MY FATHER'S DAUGHTER. HE WAS FEARLESS. SO AM I.

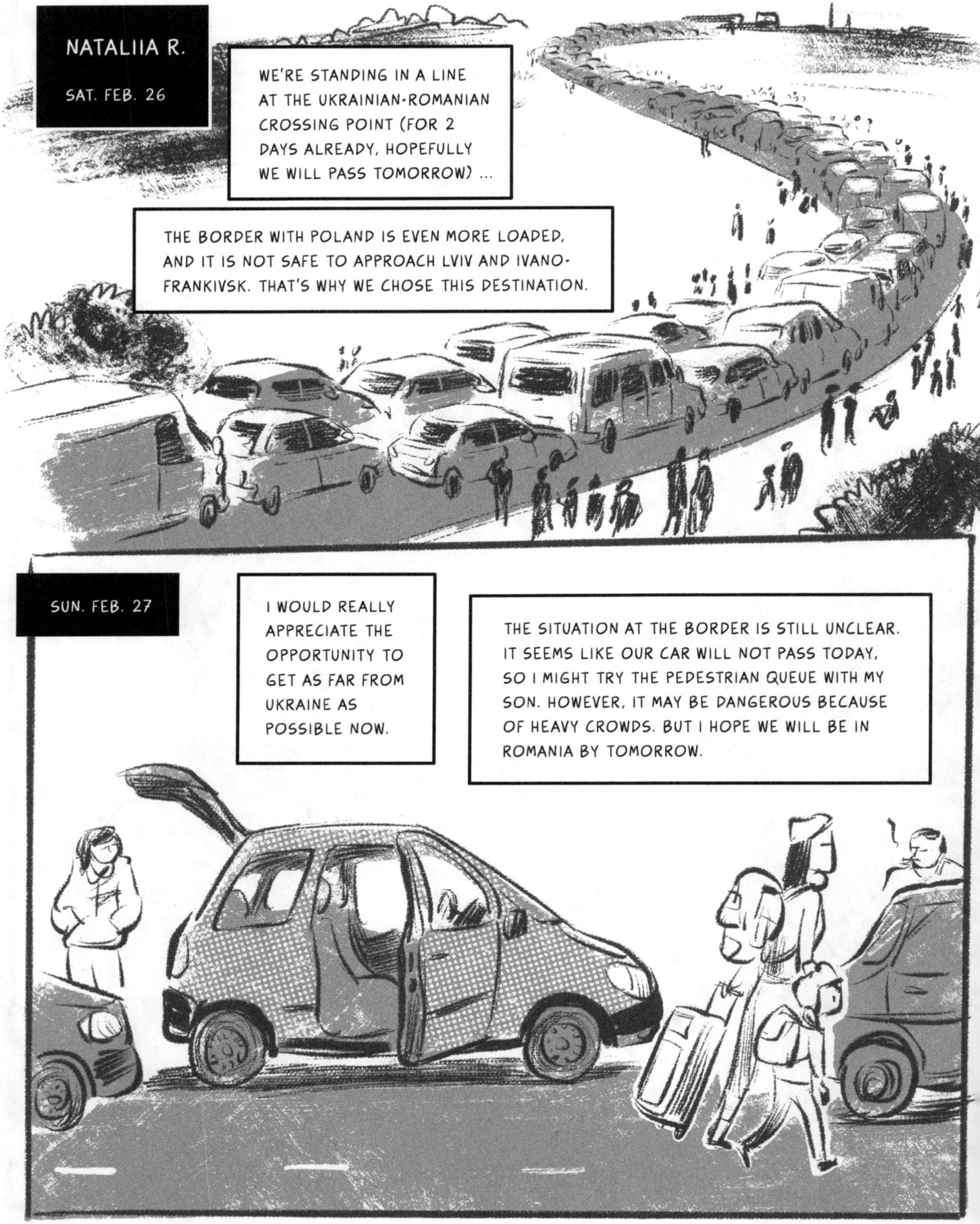
NATALIIA R.
SAT. FEB. 26
WE'RE STANDING IN A LINE AT THE UKRAINIAN-ROMANIAN CROSSING POINT (FOR 2 DAYS ALREADY, HOPEFULLY WE WILL PASS TOMORROW) ...
THE BORDER WITH POLAND IS EVEN MORE LOADED, AND IT IS NOT SAFE TO APPROACH LVIV AND IVANO-FRANKIVSK. THAT'S WHY WE CHOSE THIS DESTINATION.
SUN. FEB. 27
I WOULD REALLY APPRECIATE THE OPPORTUNITY TO GET AS FAR FROM UKRAINE AS POSSIBLE NOW.
THE SITUATION AT THE BORDER IS STILL UNCLEAR. IT SEEMS LIKE OUR CAR WILL NOT PASS TODAY, SO I MIGHT TRY THE PEDESTRIAN QUEUE WITH MY SON. HOWEVER, IT MAY BE DANGEROUS BECAUSE OF HEAVY CROWDS. BUT I HOPE WE WILL BE IN ROMANIA BY TOMORROW.

TUES. MAR. 1

I AM SO HAPPY TO TELL YOU I BOUGHT THE FLIGHT TICKETS AND EXPECT TO ARRIVE IN GOTHENBURG THERE IN SWEDEN ON THE 3RD.

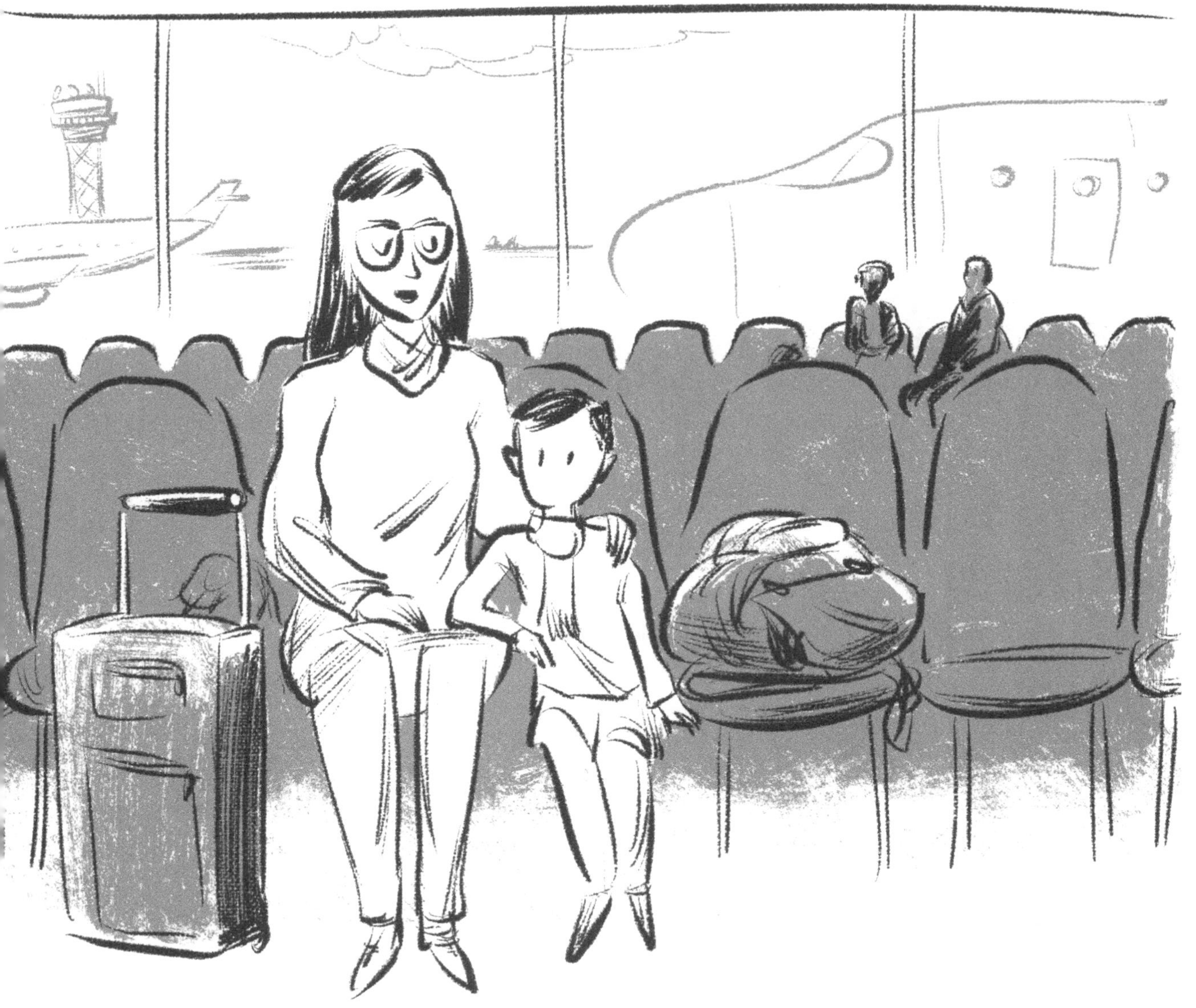

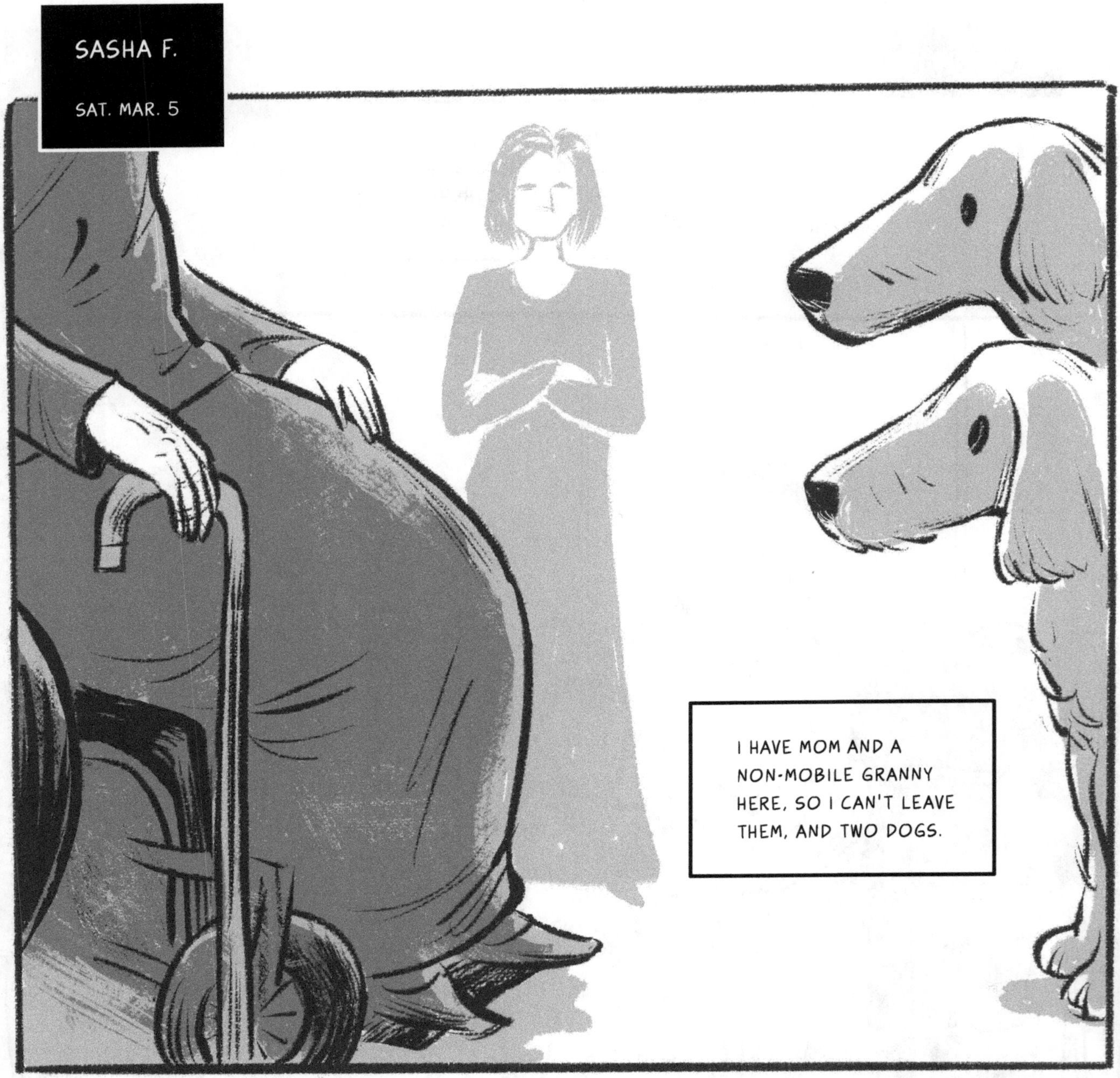
SASHA F.
SAT. MAR. 5
I HAVE MOM AND A NON-MOBILE GRANNY HERE, SO I CAN'T LEAVE THEM, AND TWO DOGS.

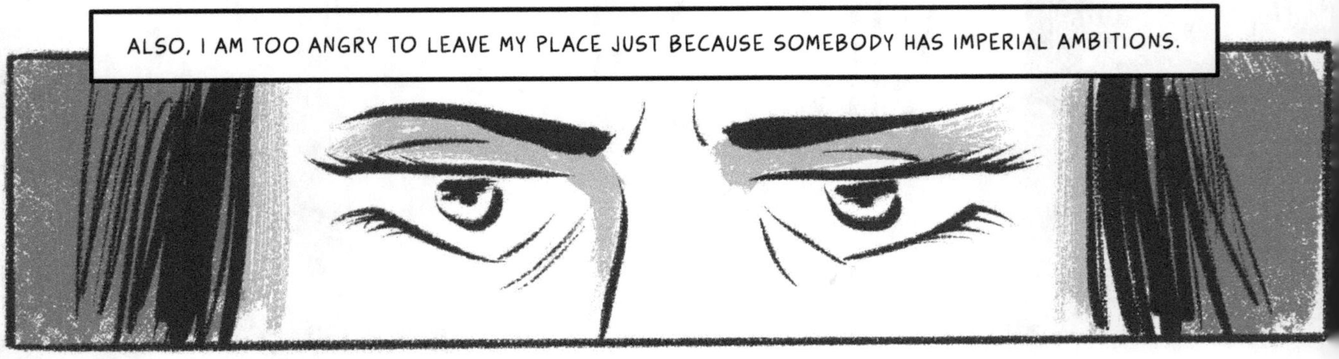
ALSO, I AM TOO ANGRY TO LEAVE MY PLACE JUST BECAUSE SOMEBODY HAS IMPERIAL AMBITIONS.

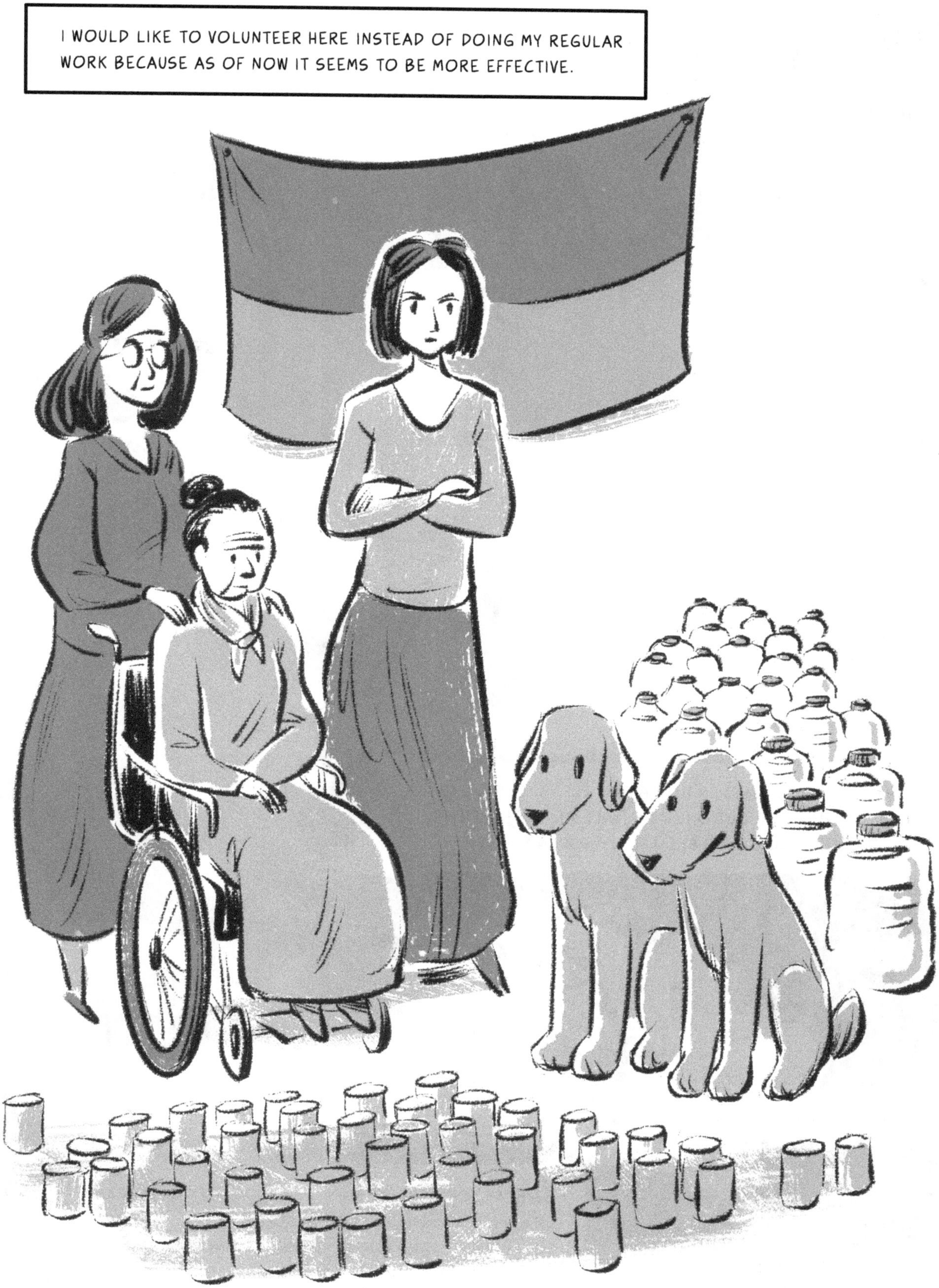
I WOULD LIKE TO VOLUNTEER HERE INSTEAD OF DOING MY REGULAR WORK BECAUSE AS OF NOW IT SEEMS TO BE MORE EFFECTIVE.

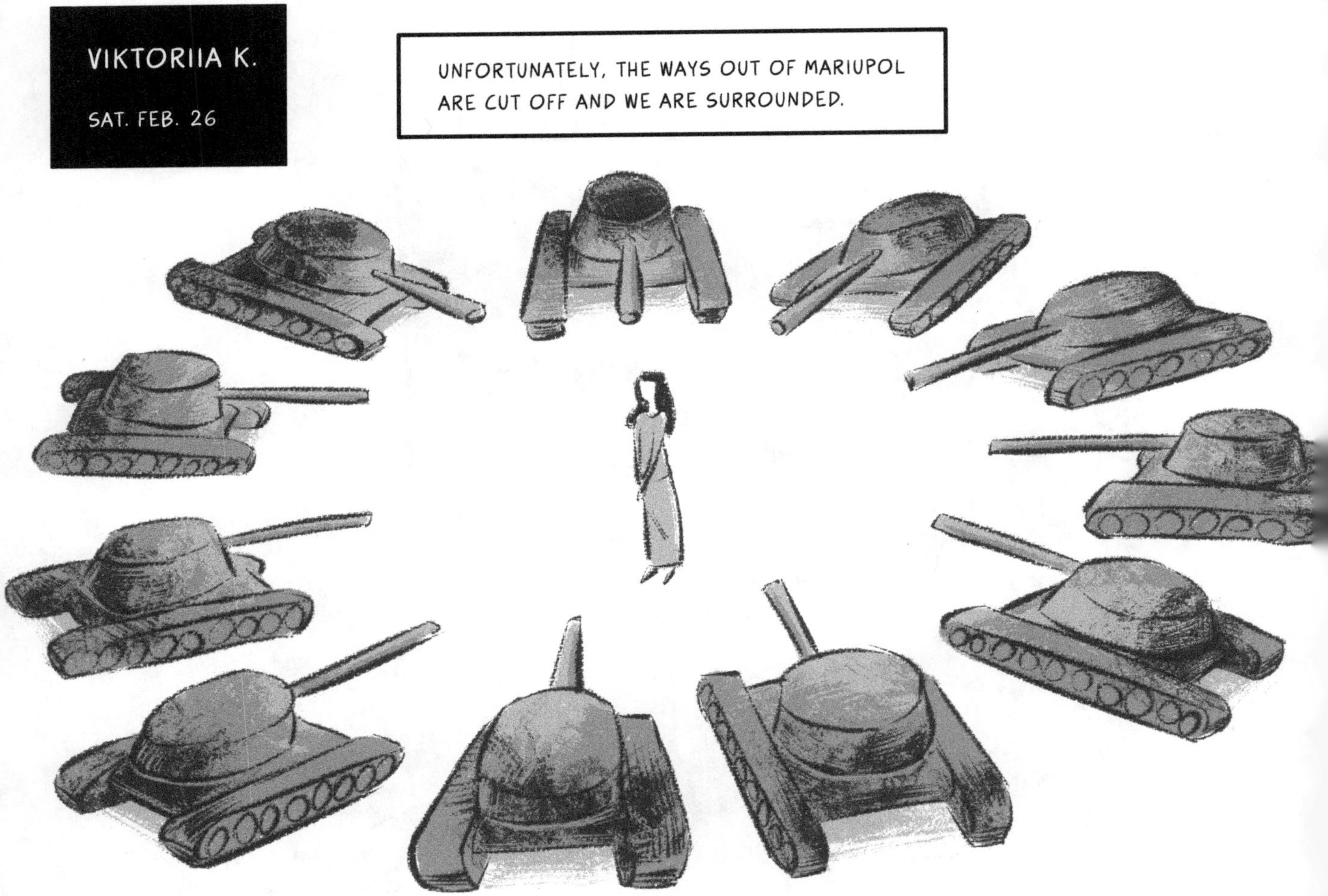
VIKTORIIA K.
SAT. FEB. 26
UNFORTUNATELY, THE WAYS OUT OF MARIUPOL ARE CUT OFF AND WE ARE SURROUNDED.

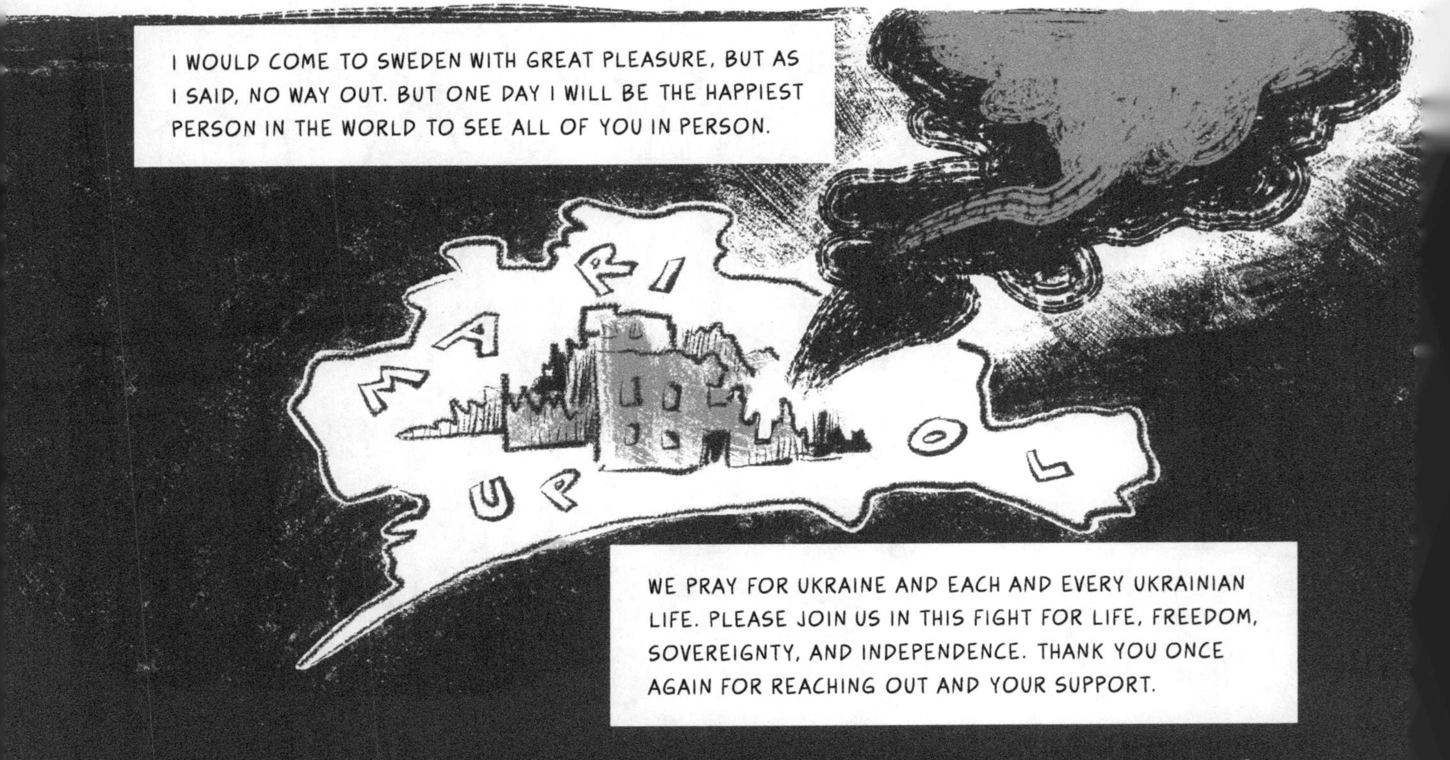
I WOULD COME TO SWEDEN WITH GREAT PLEASURE, BUT AS I SAID, NO WAY OUT. BUT ONE DAY I WILL BE THE HAPPIEST PERSON IN THE WORLD TO SEE ALL OF YOU IN PERSON.
MARIUPOL
WE PRAY FOR UKRAINE AND EACH AND EVERY UKRAINIAN LIFE. PLEASE JOIN US IN THIS FIGHT FOR LIFE, FREEDOM, SOVEREIGNTY, AND INDEPENDENCE. THANK YOU ONCE AGAIN FOR REACHING OUT AND YOUR SUPPORT.

TUES. MAR. 15

FINALLY WE MANAGED TO EVACUATE FROM MARIUPOL. NOW WE ARE ON THE WAY TO A SAFE PLACE.

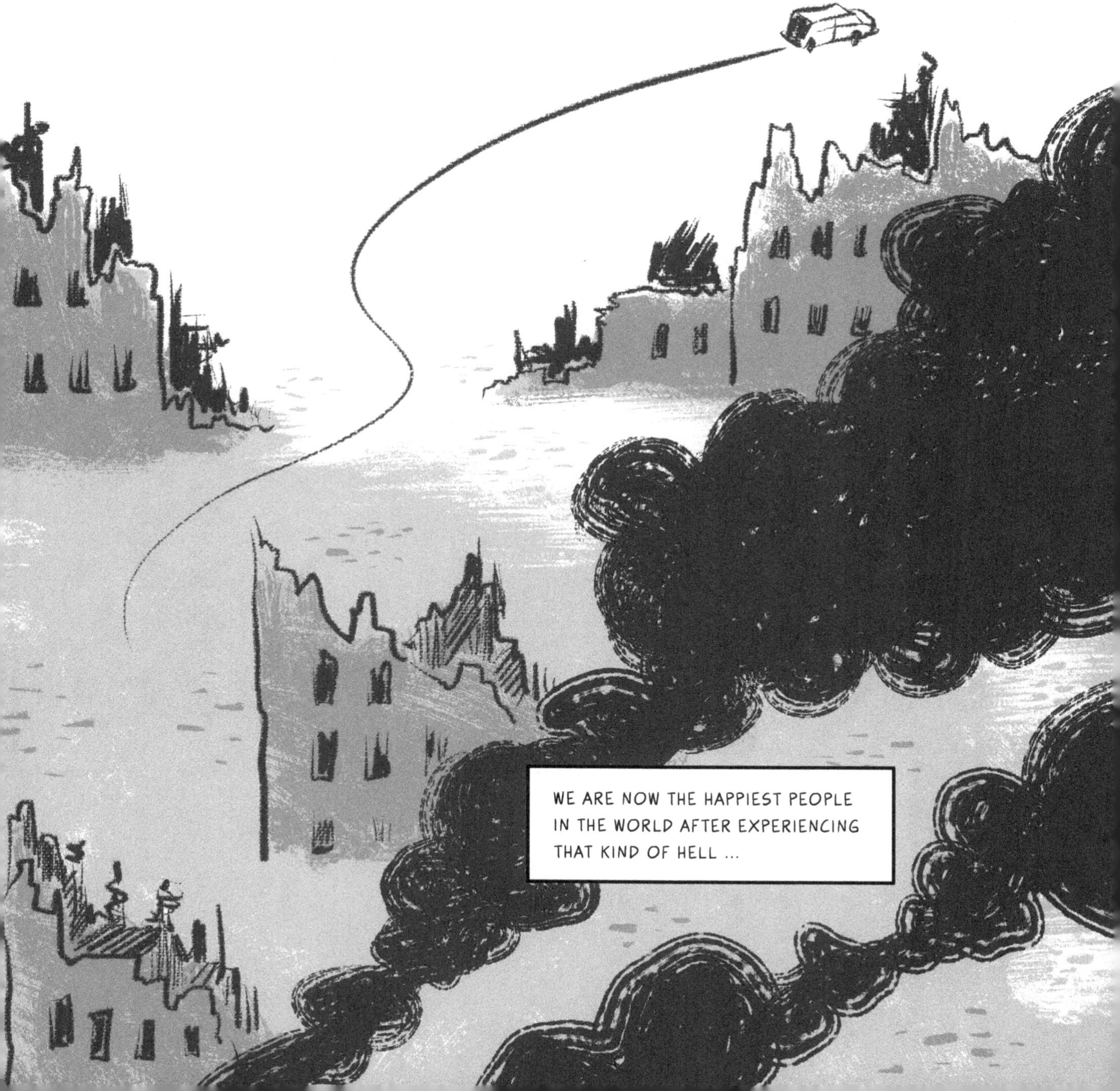
WE ARE NOW THE HAPPIEST PEOPLE IN THE WORLD AFTER EXPERIENCING THAT KIND OF HELL ...

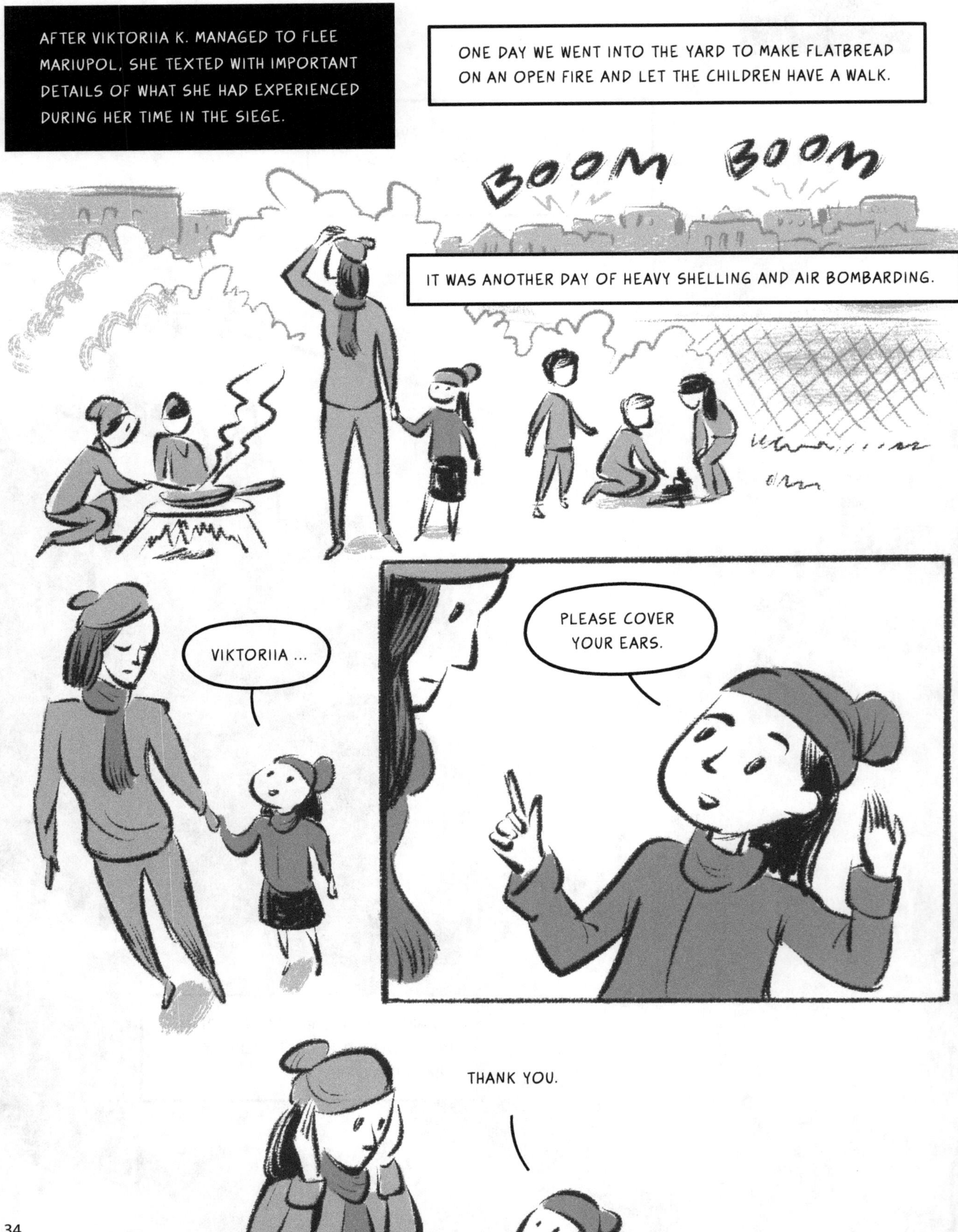
AFTER VIKTORIIA K. MANAGED TO FLEE MARIUPOL, SHE TEXTED WITH IMPORTANT DETAILS OF WHAT SHE HAD EXPERIENCED DURING HER TIME IN THE SIEGE.
ONE DAY WE WENT INTO THE YARD TO MAKE FLATBREAD ON AN OPEN FIRE AND LET THE CHILDREN HAVE A WALK.
BOOM BOOM
IT WAS ANOTHER DAY OF HEAVY SHELLING AND AIR BOMBARDING.
VIKTORIIA ...
PLEASE COVER YOUR EARS.
THANK YOU.

STOP THIS!

*Heartfelt thanks to the Swedish Institute, Keit Spiegel, Lisa Broadwell,
Karin Zelano, Carli Hansen and Janice Evans at the University of Toronto Press,
and the entire SAYP community*

Map of Ukraine

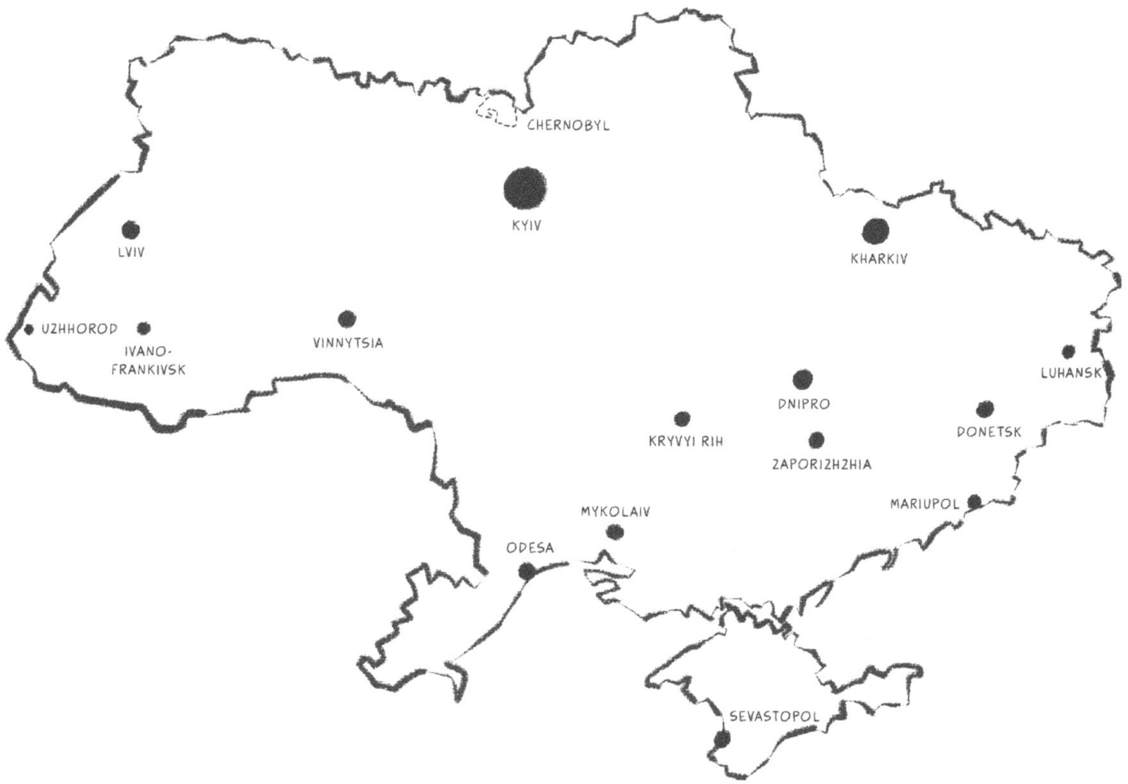
CHERNOBYL
KYIV
LVIV
KHARKIV
UZHHOROD
IVANO-
FRANKIVSK
VINNYTSIA
LUHANSK
DNIPRO
KRYVYI RIH
ZAPORIZHZHIA
DONETSK
MARIUPOL
MYKOLAIV
ODESA
SEVASTOPOL

Appendix I: Timeline of Events

Messages from Ukraine takes place in the weeks following the full-scale Russian invasion of Ukraine on February 24, 2022. The term *full-scale* is important, as in 2014 Russia had already annexed Crimea, as well as invaded the Donbas region under the guise of providing humanitarian support to pro-Russian separatists in Donetsk and Luhansk. Readers with an interest in learning more about those first years of the war, as well as the larger-scale historical processes that shaped the development of Ukraine and its relation to Russia, are advised to read Serhii Plokhy's *The Gates of Europe* (2021) or Kent DeBenedictis's *Russian "Hybrid Warfare" and the Annexation of Crimea* (2022).

Below is a timeline of events in those first weeks, focusing exclusively on the days that the individuals featured in the book sent messages.

February 24, 2022

Shortly before six o'clock in the morning, Russian president Vladimir Putin announces the start of a "special military operation" – in reality, the wide-scale invasion of Ukraine – on Russian television. Explosions are reported throughout Ukraine, and as the day unfolds, Russian air strikes on Ukrainian air bases, military infrastructure, and other key positions take place. Russian troops cross the Ukrainian border from the east, north, and south. Ukrainian president Volodymyr Zelensky declares martial law, calling upon all able-bodied Ukrainians to take part in the defense of Ukraine, and states that Russia is on a "path of evil."

Katerina P. messages from just outside of Kyiv, saying she hopes to live through the air strikes.

February 25, 2022

Russian forces advance on Kyiv, with heavy fighting reported in the northern outskirts and suburbs. Late in the day, Ukrainian authorities confirm that Russian soldiers have taken control of Hostomel Airport, just ten kilometers (six miles) outside of the city. Residents of Kyiv converge on the capital's central railway station, trying to make their way onto trains heading west. Ukrainian guards are forced to fire blanks to disperse the crowds.

Taisiia D. messages to say that she is fleeing from the north of the city. Viktoria L. makes contact to say that she is safely abroad, having been on a work assignment.

February 26, 2022

The battle for Kyiv intensifies, with large explosions reported southwest of the city. Residents of the capital are urged to take shelter in preparation for air strikes. Russian cruise missiles strike the Black Sea coast. The United Nations Refugee Agency (UNHCR) reports that over 120,000 Ukrainians have fled the country since February 24 and warns that up to four million people could cross borders.

Almost half of the group send messages on this day. Some are committed to staying put and providing humanitarian support or joining the military, some are making plans to leave the country, and some are stuck at crowded border crossings, while others are unable to flee Kyiv given the ongoing fighting.

February 27, 2022

Satellite images show a large Russian military convoy north of Kyiv, advancing toward the city. The convoy will eventually be estimated at sixty-five kilometers (forty miles) in length. Ukrainian forces continue to hold Kyiv and are able to prevent Russian forces from gaining control of Ukraine's second-largest city, Kharkiv, located in the east. The Ukrainian Ministry of the Interior announces that 352 Ukrainian civilians have been killed in the fighting so far, with nearly 1,700 more wounded. The European Union announces that it will finance the purchase and delivery of weapons and equipment to Ukraine.

Several more messages arrive. Some of the group remain stuck at the border, as the numbers seeking to flee Ukraine grow. Others are not yet able to flee Kyiv and wait in bomb shelters, sending photos and trying to remain upbeat. Still others who are abroad as part of the Ukrainian diaspora attempt to stay in contact with family members in Ukraine and consider the most appropriate course of action.

February 28, 2022

Rocket attacks launched by Russia against Kharkiv result in multiple deaths. Blasts are reported in Mariupol. US defense officials confirm that Russian military strikes are taking place against civilian targets, but it remains uncertain whether the targeting is intentional. Ukrainian Railways announces additional trains on the route connecting Lviv with Chełm, Poland. Seating preference is given to women and the elderly.

Taisiia D. messages from Kyiv to say that she is in an air raid shelter. Olga I. has finally managed to flee Kyiv and is on the train to Lviv, where she plans to take stock of her next steps.

March 1, 2022

Kharkiv continues to suffer from heavy bombing as Russian missiles hit both residential and administrative areas in the city center. Various Kyiv neighborhoods are also reported to be under attack, including the area near the Kyiv International Airport (Zhuliany). President Zelensky declares, "Nobody will forgive. Nobody will forget." European Commission officials indicate that the EC is likely to implement the Temporary Protection Directive (European Commission, 2022), allowing Ukrainians to reside in the European Union for an initial one-year period (and potentially up to three years) without filing an asylum claim.

Nataliia R. messages to say that she will be coming to Sweden with her son. Lisa C. is in touch from Estonia to ask for assistance with procuring large quantities of foodstuffs to be transported to Ukraine.

March 3, 2022

Ukrainian and Russian government delegations meet in Belarus for negotiations. Ukrainian representatives state that the issues on the agenda are an immediate cease-fire, an armistice, and the establishment of humanitarian corridors to allow for the evacuation of Ukrainian locations that have come under shelling. Russian forces control administrative buildings in the Black Sea port city of Kherson. Odesa prepares for a Russian assault by sea.

Olga M. messages to say that she is looking into relocating her daughter and cat, though it is unclear to where.

March 4, 2022

The European Commission formally adopts the Temporary Protection Directive. Over 1.3 million Ukrainians have now left the country since February 24. A few are in the process of returning – chiefly those who were temporarily abroad at the time of the full-scale invasion, or who were part of the Ukrainian diaspora. Russian forces attack the Zaporizhzhia nuclear power plant on the shore of the Dnipro River.

Viktoria L., who had been working in Kyrgyzstan for UNICEF, is relocated to Moldova to assist Ukrainian refugees crossing the border. Solomia H. writes to say that she is at the Ukrainian-Slovakian border.

March 5, 2022

The situation in Mariupol continues to deteriorate. A cease-fire that had been brokered is violated by Russian forces who resume shelling, forcing local authorities to stop planned evacuations. Residents of Irpin, looking to flee the outlying district near the capital, are forced to navigate a treacherous path over damaged and destroyed bridge infrastructure. Residents of the southern city of Kherson, now under Russian occupation, stage street protests against the occupying forces, waving Ukrainian flags and chanting.

Sasha F. sends a message saying that she has no plans to leave Kyiv and hopes to take part in volunteer efforts. She is emphatic about not being forced out of the country by the Russian military.

March 9, 2022

President Zelensky says that a Russian air strike has destroyed a maternity hospital in the besieged city of Mariupol. According to Ukrainian Foreign Minister Dmytro Kuleba, conditions in the city are "apocalyptic." Attempts to evacuate one hundred thousand Ukrainians from locations nationwide result in forty thousand successful evacuations. Thousands of thermal blankets and mattresses transported from Poland to Lviv on March 8 are now in place, allowing for increased capacity in the city's internally displaced persons (IDP) reception centers. The Kyiv Classic Orchestra performs the Ukrainian national anthem for passersby in Lyiv's Maidan Square.

Taisiia D. messages to say that she has arrived in Lviv from Kyiv.

March 15, 2022

The State Emergency Service of Ukraine reports that Russian shelling of Kyiv during the day has resulted in multiple fires. Over three million Ukrainians have now fled the country since February 24. Local officials in Mariupol say that 350,000 of the city's 540,000 inhabitants remain trapped in the besieged city. Russian troops seize a hospital in the city late in the day and take roughly five hundred people hostage. Two thousand cars are able to leave the city with evacuees.

After nearly two weeks of no contact, Viktoriia K. sends a message, saying that she was among those who managed to be evacuated from Mariupol.

Appendix II: Interview with the Authors

Who are the people in this book?

The individuals featured in this book are all young professionals from Ukraine whose work centers on migration and integration. Almost all of them had taken part in a two-week training module on migration and integration challenges, organized by the University of Gothenburg, Sweden, as part of the Swedish Institute Academy for Young Professionals (SAYP) program.

Their professional backgrounds and current occupations are quite varied. Some have been working or volunteering for Ukrainian civil society organizations that provide support to internally displaced Ukrainians from the Donbas region. Many have been working with leading international organizations – such as the United Nations Refugee Agency (UNHCR), the UN International Organization of Migration (IOM), and the UN Children's Fund (UNICEF) – on issues of refugee reception, settlement, and integration. Still others are in academia, teaching and researching at Ukrainian universities, completing postgraduate degrees abroad, or completing degrees in Ukraine. Some have previously worked for the Ukrainian state administration and have a keen interest in the legal challenges faced by internally displaced Ukrainians. They are joined in the program by young professionals from other Eastern Partnership and Baltic Sea Region countries.

What unites them as a group is not just their shared interest in migration and integration, but their ongoing connection to the SAYP program. The two-week program is intensive, with an emphasis on group work and plans for continued cooperation. This close relationship is sustained by annual follow-up projects, allowing the alumni to further develop their skill sets and engage in knowledge transfer about migration and integration issues. The result is that participants in these annual cohorts get to know one another quite well: staying actively involved as alumni, spreading the word to potential applicants, and often developing close friendships with one another. As we say, SAYP is a family.

Who are you, and what is your connection to the people in the book?

Gregg is a professor of public administration at the University of Gothenburg in Sweden and has been organizing this SAYP module since 2018. Joonas is an illustrator and graphic novelist in Estonia. Our collaboration began as part of the SAYP 2020 follow-up project, which stemmed from Gregg's growing interests in autoethnography and comics-based research. Gregg asked young migration professionals to write short autoethnographic vignettes about their workplace experiences that would then form the basis for an anthology of graphic short stories. Several Ukrainian alumni were involved in this project, receiving training in vignette writing and developing storyboards for the graphic stories.

Joonas became involved as part of a happy accident. When the initial illustrator for the project withdrew, Gregg did a bit of searching that immediately led to Joonas. The bold and clean visual style of his previous graphic novel held enormous appeal, as did his work collaborating with Estonian journalists on an exhibition project. It was a cold-call approach, and a few Zoom meetings later it was apparent that we shared enthusiasm for a collaborative venture in which we would both be pushing ourselves beyond our professional comfort zones, but with the support of other project members who had complementary skills and commitment to the concept.

How did the start of the full-scale war change your plans?

February 24, 2022, the day that Russia launched its full-scale invasion of Ukraine, changed everything in ways big and small. Of course, our thoughts were immediately preoccupied with the events that were unfolding and the surrounding uncertainty. We were especially concerned about our friends and contacts in Ukraine – those who were involved in the book project that was underway, the overall group of nearly twenty-five alumni who had been involved in the program over the years, and Ukrainians that we had met through training sessions that our alumni had organized.

Initially, we pushed aside all thoughts of consequences that the war held for the book project. Everyday concerns like project timelines suddenly felt quite unimportant. What did feel important was trying to overcome that sense of powerlessness in the face of this horrible act of aggression, and to identify ways that we could help. Organizers of SAYP modules at other Swedish universities had already been developing plans to assist Ukrainian module alumni and others with coming to Sweden via Poland, should they wish to do so. Since Gregg had been communicating with several of the Ukrainian alumni online in the days leading up to February 24, this seemed like a natural way to reach out to them with a concrete offer of assistance.

How did this lead to your work on *Messages from Ukraine*?

Well, the messages from the Ukrainian alumni began rolling in. They were a mix in terms of the level of detail, and also in terms of people's current status and their plans for the immediate future. Gregg made a spreadsheet with contact details and updated information about each of the alumni so that he could have an overview of whether they had been in touch, where they were, and what options they might be considering in terms of staying put, relocating within Ukraine (becoming an IDP), or seeking refuge abroad.

It was difficult to read the messages without trying to imagine what these people were experiencing. When someone messages you briefly and says that they are fleeing Kyiv on a train with a gerbil, what does that moment look like? When somebody else messages you and assures you that they are okay, but are trying to procure medical supplies and have attached a list, what does that flurry of work and logistics look like? Gregg began to consider each of the messages not just in light of what the person said, but how he imagined their experiences. It was for him, after some reflection, part of a sensemaking process: trying to understand what was happening to his colleagues abroad.

We began discussing these messages and how each text could be regarded as a type of vignette that conveyed a moment in time. Ethical considerations were paramount at this stage. It would have been completely inappropriate to contact each individual and ask for additional information about what they were experiencing at that moment. At the same time, the messages presented an interesting opportunity. Since we were already collaborating with SAYP alumni on a graphic anthology, it seemed natural to think about putting these messages into a similar format.

How did you approach this work?

This book is informed by scholarship celebrating the impressionistic nature of interpretive research, embracing its ability to produce "a stylized rather than faithful representation … conveying vivid, rich details that best capture what the researchers deem to be the most important features" (Boswell & Corbett, 2015, p. 220). We believe that visual methods are especially well-suited to achieving this. Many have discussed the value of integrating visual images into the research process; for example, Weber (2008) has observed that "images can be used to capture the ineffable. Some things just need to be shown, not merely stated. Artistic images can help us access those elusive, hard-to-put-into-words aspects of knowledge that might otherwise remain hidden or ignored" (p. 44).

We believe that there is, quite simply, "no objective, detached social scientist providing an authoritative representation of what happened" (Rhodes, 2014, p. 325). To that end, by adding to text images that interpret the moment from the perspective of the recipient, visual methods allow us to "objectify immediate experience" (Boswell & Corbett, 2015, p. 219). Joonas's illustration style aligns particularly well with an impressionistic approach to interpretive research: sacrificing certain details to better capture a mood (Boswell

& Corbett, 2015). His approach to comics makes use of a relatively sparse style in which visual details are limited, with the result being that his images call attention to key parts of the messages, and evoke both setting and emotion. In the service of inviting the reader to consider an overall mood and to identify more immediately with the situations being portrayed, the conscious sacrifice of some details serves an important function in this work. Of course, we are far behind the vanguard that has adopted comics in the service of social science research. Within migration studies, there are some excellent and inspiring examples, such as the online migration comics included in the PositiveNegatives project (Burrell & Hörschelmann, 2019). However, there hasn't yet been the emergence of a critical mass of comics-based scholars within migration studies, such as that already found in the medical humanities (Czerwiec et al., 2015).

At the end of the day, we "can only offer interpretations of interpretations" (Needham, 2015, p. 340), telling "stories about other people's stories" (Bevir & Rhodes, 2003, p. 133). By using comics to cast new light on contexts central to war, (im)mobility, and resilience, we hope that this book contributes to comics-based research being seen as a valuable approach and further integrated into migration studies.

If we shift from the big-picture issues of approach to the nuts and bolts of preparing the comic, what was your workflow?

We definitely benefited from collaborating with each other over the past couple of years. Yet we had still not met face-to-face, even as we worked on the final draft of this book. The bulk of our communication took the form of email, cloud storage links, and the occasional online meeting. Once we decided to develop the text messages into a project of its own, Gregg began by reviewing all the messages he received from the alumni and choosing the ones that had left a particularly strong impression on him at the time of reading. These were not always the most dramatic or event-filled accounts, just messages that had a significant quality to them somehow, be it the drama of war, the everyday mundanity of war, the absurdity of war, or the uncertainty that was part and parcel of messages with limited information. Gregg then prepared a basic text file that included the full set of messages each person had sent, with selections that seemed like particularly good candidates for inclusion highlighted in bold, and detailed suggestions for accompanying images, often down to the individual panel level.

Joonas then produced preliminary sketches based on this text file, but he was not limited to the highlighted portions of the messages or the specific suggestions that Gregg had made for the images. Joonas had been deeply moved by the events of the war and felt a close attachment to the Ukrainians, which certainly shaped his own impressions of how the messages could be portrayed. Gregg's notes helped Joonas a great deal in terms of providing the overall direction, allowing the images to fall into place mostly on their own. This is a central part of the collaboration. Joonas was emphatically not restricted to the role of an illustrator who was executing a brief provided by Gregg, but was an equal coauthor, with shared responsibility for making decisions big and small about the individual narratives and how they would be presented to the reader. Once the preliminary sketches were prepared, we discussed them via email, with an eye toward clearing up any miscommunications, considering where more or less detail would best serve the message, and deciding whether the text from the message itself was appropriately divided among frames.

One point that we revisited several times was how much we should correct spelling and grammar in the text messages, all of which had been written in English. While every one of the individuals featured in the book is highly proficient in English, their messages did contain some errors and fragments. This was only natural, given that they were often sending quick messages under tense, stressful conditions – not to mention the casual nature of text messaging. While we wanted to preserve the authenticity of the messages as written, clarity ultimately prevailed, and we opted for standard usages.

Another key issue that we considered was how to order the presentation of the individuals and their messages in the book. We accepted early on that there was no single way to resolve this. We knew that we wanted the reader to encounter certain themes and experiences prior to others, and that presenting the messages in chronological order (to the extent possible) would prevent us from being able to do so. For example, we consciously wanted the reader to encounter Olga M. first, as her messages introduce the reader to the ambiguity that was frequently inherent in these texts. When Olga wrote that she planned to stay at home and help the army by volunteering, did she mean through civilian support or by picking up a gun? This section is then followed by that of Olga I., who represents a contrast in terms of her decision to flee Kyiv for Lviv, an evacuation route likely known to many readers. The messages from both Roman H. and Katerina P., while among the earliest sent, are placed later in the book. In each case, they present a contrast with the decision made by the person in the previous section. Oleksii V. is focused on the complexities of supply procurement, while Roman H. is thinking of the importance of staying and fighting. Mariia L. is attempting to pack and flee with her son, while Katerina P. does not have that possibility. Finally, we end the book with Viktoriia K. We had been especially worried about her during the two-week period in which she did not respond to Gregg's messages. The horrors of the Mariupol siege are broadly known, making Viktoriia's messages about the importance of Ukraine's struggle, her eventual escape, and the actions of a little girl especially powerful and poignant.

How involved in this process were the people who appear in the book?

We completed the draft pages before sharing the details of the project with those whose messages are included, knowing that obtaining their consent would be an absolute necessity. Given the stress they were under, we didn't want to overwhelm them with messages. We knew our seed of an idea was not their most pressing concern at that time. Gregg had read several posts on social media from Ukrainian colleagues who expressed appreciation for receiving messages of support but pointed out that there simply wasn't time to respond to each and every one, given the day-to-day reality of the war. We also wanted to get a feel for how the idea would take shape. So, it was only once we had a set of advanced sketches that we contacted the individuals.

We shared the details of the project and copies of the pages, and requested feedback, with the aim of getting consent from all involved. The responses were unanimously positive, which gave us the green light to keep developing the book. Moreover, we were energized by the enthusiastic, encouraging tone of their responses. Many of the individuals wrote that they viewed the book as an important way to keep the public spotlight on the everyday experiences of Ukrainians whose lives were dramatically upended by the full-scale war in those first two weeks. Several pointed out what they regarded as a realistic portrayal of their experiences. One person told us how important it was to see that her pet was included. All told, this made us feel confident not only that we had their support, but that we had a shared vision of the project.

As authors, we both felt strongly that we would not be writing this book for personal gain. We see it as a contribution to keeping a public spotlight on the war. We aim to honor those in the book, and the millions of others who have had to face similar hardships and make excruciating decisions.

Did any of the people involved ask you to alter how their messages were being portrayed?

In two cases, individuals asked whether it would be possible to make changes to the draft sketches, but for quite different reasons. Anastasiia T. contacted Gregg to share details about what had actually happened after she sent her initial messages. In her first round of messages, she had written that she was studying in Vienna but would return to Ukraine and fight if need be, framing herself as the fearless daughter of a fearless father. When she contacted Gregg after seeing the draft sketches, she explained that she actually wound up choosing a very different course of action. Rather than deciding to return to Ukraine and take up arms, she became actively involved in organizing against the Russian invasion through protests and other anti-war initiatives in Vienna. As such, Anastasiia wanted to know if we would be willing to redraft her pages to reflect what *actually* transpired. However, this didn't turn out to be necessary, as she understood that the aim of the book was to highlight the points in time in which the messages were written, and not how circumstances ultimately played out.

In another case, we opted to give an extra two pages to one of the individuals. Viktoriia K., who had been in Mariupol during the initial period of the siege, contacted Gregg after she saw the first sketches for her two pages and shared a moment from the siege when she had been outdoors with some of the children for whom she was responsible. Her description was brief but the details were easy to visualize, especially the child who felt it was necessary to warn Viktoriia before yelling at Russian aircraft. We discussed Viktoriia's message and some suggestions for the sketches, and we agreed that the informal principle guiding the book up to that point – two pages per participant – did not need to be followed at the expense of excluding important moments. The decision to provide the additional two pages for Viktoriia's messages was made easier not only by the emotional resonance of the events being described, but also by the precedent set by others engaged in comics-based research. Indeed, one of the genuine advantages of working in this vein is the number of articles published by scholars explaining their own comics-based research processes. While not step-by-step how-to manuals, such articles provide important glimpses into what goes on behind the scenes as researchers confront challenges in designing, adapting, and implementing comics-based research strategies (e.g., Cancellieri & Peterle, 2021; Forde, 2021; Meer & Müller, 2021). These were important resources to have at hand, providing some confidence that a certain flexibility would best serve the aims of the book.

How does the book shed light on the topic of migration, particularly as related to wartime experiences?

As a result of the war, most of the people featured in this book shifted from developing and administering migration and integration measures to becoming people targeted by these measures. In several cases, individuals working with IDP issues suddenly found themselves abroad as refugees. In other cases, refugee specialists working with international organizations in Ukraine suddenly became IDPs seeking a safe location elsewhere in the country. Of course, this is common for any person in a war – one's formal role and category changes, often becoming dual or even multiple. But it opens up an especially interesting line of inquiry for the eventual day the war is over, when these Ukrainian migration and integration professionals may begin to reflect on what it was like to be on the other side of the table. Was there a "professional" voice in the back of their heads, evaluating what they were experiencing and taking notes for the future? What stood out to them in terms of their professional roles?

The book also highlights the everyday manner in which agency is exercised by individuals confronted with the sudden and dramatic possibility of becoming migrants: assessments of whether to stay or go, whether to become a refugee or an IDP, what destinations are seen as possible choices, and how one can grapple with feelings of disempowerment in the new setting. Migrant agency is, of course, not an absolute, but it exists within certain social contexts (Borrelli et al., 2021). However, as we reflected on the messages and began reviewing preliminary sketches, it was often apparent that even in conditions of war – where choices are often substantially limited – agency was visibly present, and that individuals were not passively waiting for circumstances or actors to dictate specific choices they would make.

For example, Solomia H.'s decision to relocate to the Ukrainian-Slovakian border is especially interesting, suggesting a strategy of balancing personal safety with a reluctance to flee abroad. On the one hand, her decision underscores a desire to be in a comparatively safe location, one that had largely avoided coming under wide-scale Russian attack. Yet her decision to travel only as far as the Ukrainian border city of Uzhhorod is significant. To cross the border would have put Solomia abroad, as a refugee outside of Ukraine. But she hoped that there would be no need to leave. By staying in Uzhhorod, Solomia was able to exercise some degree of control over the situation: safety for the moment, the chance to remain on Ukrainian soil, and the ability to flee over the border if necessary.

By contrast, Nataliia R. evaluated the security risk to herself and her son as requiring a very different solution: that of going abroad and opting for temporary protection in Sweden. Without providing much detail of specific events, Nataliia nonetheless made it clear that she was uncomfortable not just with remaining in Ukraine, but with relocating to those countries bordering Ukraine where millions were already fleeing. Sweden provided Nataliia with a sense of safety, partly on the basis of its distance from Ukraine.

Agency is not something we witnessed only in those who chose to flee to other parts of Ukraine or abroad. For Lisa C., a Ukrainian living in Estonia as a student migrant, agency was explicit in her decision to remain in Estonia and take part in coordinating large-scale humanitarian supply efforts from abroad. Throughout her time in Estonia, Lisa had been involved in initiatives to assist Ukrainian IDPs from Donbas through various networks and NGOs. Indeed, Lisa was herself an IDP from the Donbas region before relocating to Estonia, and engaging in this type of humanitarian assistance was already a core part of her professional identity while in Kyiv. Lisa could have made the decision that many Ukrainians abroad did at the start of the war – to return to Ukraine. Alternatively, she could have chosen to relocate to a border country to provide on-site humanitarian assistance. Yet, in Lisa's case, agency led her not to a break with the past or a new course of action, but rather to a conscious continuation along the path already chosen. Highly experienced in logistics work for the provision of aid and supplies from abroad, she did not need to relocate for safety or to continue supporting Ukraine at the outbreak of the full-scale war.

As a final example, Sasha F.'s messages provide a glimpse into a case where there were real constraints in terms of leaving: family members, including a grandmother with mobility issues, and two pet dogs, meant that leaving Kyiv was not on the table. However, her messages indicate that the decision to remain was not based solely on the need to be a caregiver. By staying put, Sasha sought to symbolically show Russia that she, like many other Ukrainians, would not be intimidated. More explicitly linked to an expression of agency was her decision to put her regular employment on hold, and to devote her time to volunteer humanitarian initiatives. Agency is a real thing, both for those who choose to migrate during times of war and for those who choose to stay. It is present in the everyday actions and decisions of the people in this book.

What sort of impact do you hope the book will have?

This war has produced the largest refugee event in Europe since World War II. While each story is unique, millions of Ukrainians have experiences that are instantly recognizable as part of the narrative of war – the refugee in search of safety, the civilian ready to fight, the volunteer looking to make a difference. The messages from the people in this book moved us both very deeply. We believe that their words will have a similar impact on a much broader public and that there is value in sharing them. In the opening days of the war, several of our Ukrainian colleagues regularly stressed on social media the many types of support that were acutely needed, particularly those focusing on fundraising for humanitarian and military supplies, as well as those coordinating support for Ukrainian refugees in search of transport and housing. But they also stressed the importance of initiatives that would keep public attention focused on the war. We view this book as a modest contribution to highlighting the impact of the war by showcasing the impressive resilience of our Ukrainian SAYP alumni.

We also hope the book will be of value in the classroom, particularly for students with an interest in qualitative research methods. When comics are included as a resource, students can encounter a specific and relatable form of narrative inquiry that allows them to grapple with "what it means to interpret and experience the world (rather than explain or predict it), both from the perspective of scholars and the people they study" (Ospina & Dodge, 2005, p. 144). Indeed, when Gregg presented a preliminary draft of the book at a seminar for colleagues, one person suggested that the messages served as an ideal opportunity for students to consider the process of how subject viewpoints in research are represented more generally, and also alternate framings of the messages contained in the book more specifically. Works of comics-based research such as this book can help students think about their own subjectivity as researchers, and how it is compounded by collaborating with others who may use a different set of research practices (Kuttner at al., 2021). There is, of course, no one way to manage the issue of researcher subjectivity, be it in comics-based research or any other type of research. However, we confront the issue head-on at the start of this book, making researcher subjectivity central to the presentation of each set of messages. We view this approach – presenting messages that contain limited information, together with our own interpretations – as a strategy for achieving an open-ended, but still plausible, framing of experiences. We invite students to consider this book as one example of how arts-based research can be carried out fruitfully, and how the worldviews of the social science researcher and the artist can meet and inform one another in the process of creating a shared product (Finley, 2008).

Appendix III: Study Guide

If you are interested in talking about the individuals in the book as characters:

1 Which of the individuals are you interested in knowing more about and why?
2 Is there a specific person in the book with whom you identify? Why or why not?
3 Do you agree with all of the choices made by the individuals in the book? Is there anyone you think should have behaved differently? Or that you wish had behaved differently? Who and why?
4 From whose story do you feel you learn the most about the war? In what way?
5 Which experience portrayed in the book is the most unexpected to you and why?

If you are interested in migration and mobility:

1 Should we understand the different choices made by the individuals in the book – to stay, to become an IDP, to go abroad, or to return home – as long-term or short-term choices? Can you imagine circumstances in which individuals who made one decision about staying or going might suddenly make another?
2 Two of the individuals in the book are part of the Ukrainian diaspora. Do you think living abroad when one's country is attacked leads a person to have perceptions or attitudes regarding the nation and national identity that differ from those held by people who haven't emigrated?
3 Migration has been called a gendered phenomenon. How is gender relevant when considering the migration choices made by the individuals in the book?
4 Apart from gender, how might age and professional background shape the options available to the individuals in the book? How might other individuals have more or fewer options?

5 Pets are prominent characters in several stories in the book. Why do you think the individuals place such importance on their pets when making plans to stay or go during wartime?

6 What do we learn about migration during wartime by focusing on brief moments in people's everyday lives?

If you are interested in comics:

1 How do you think the illustrations provide important contextual detail that isn't present in the messages themselves? What are some specific examples?

2 Some people would argue that each page and panel needs to be filled with the maximum amount of detail in order to make it realistic. Others would say that less is more. Which approach do you think is more effective and why?

3 Would the mood of the book be any different if the pages had been in color? What do you see as the advantages and disadvantages of using black-and-white illustrations?

4 With one exception, the book makes use of two pages per individual. Would you have chosen a different strategy? If you had more pages to devote to each person, what sort of visual information would you include? What sort of text?

If you are interested in qualitative research methods:

1 How can you make use of comics-based research in your own work, such as your undergraduate, MA, or PhD thesis?

2 How would you persuade a skeptic that comics-based research has something to offer when addressing research topics in your own field?

3 What other visual methods do you see as possibilities for researching topics in your field?

4 If you primarily conduct social science research, how would you go about collaborating with a researcher from the humanities to develop an interesting project in your field? If you conduct research within the humanities, how would you go about collaborating with a social scientist?

If you don't like to answer questions, but prefer to do things:

1 Make a list of the things you would take with you if you suddenly had to flee your home and had only a short time to pack one small bag. Explain why you made your specific choices.

2 Choose messages from one person in the book that you would illustrate differently. You can either draw new pages or write a description of what would be pictured.

3 Pick a different cover image for the book, and write a short statement justifying your choice.

4 Pretend that you have to organize refugee reception in your hometown. Write a short memo describing the ideal way the plan should be carried out. Develop specific tasks, and be sure to include a list of public, private, and nonprofit actors that would need to be involved.

References

Bevir, M., & Rhodes, R.A.W. (2003). *Interpreting British governance*. Psychology Press.

Borrelli, L., Pinkerton, P., Safouane, H., Jünemann, A., Göttsche, S., Scheel, S., & C. Oelgemöller. (2021). Agency within mobility. *Geopolitics, 27*(4), 1140–1167. https://doi.org/10.1080/14650045.2021.1973733

Boswell, J., & Corbett, J. (2015). Embracing impressionism: Revealing the brush strokes of interpretive research. *Critical Policy Studies, 9*(2), 216–225. https://doi.org/10.1080/19460171.2014.971039

Burrell, K., & Hörschelmann, K. (2019). Perilous journeys: Visualising the racialised "refugee crisis." *Antipode: A Radical Journal of Geography, 51*(1), 45–65. https://doi.org/10.1111/anti.12429

Cancellieri, A., & Peterle, G. (2021). Urban research in comics form: Exploring spaces, agency and narrative maps in Italian marginalized neighbourhoods. *Sociologica: International Journal for Sociological Debate, (15)*1, 211–239. https://doi.org/10.6092/issn.1971-8853/12776

Czerwiec, M.K., Williams, I., Squier, S.M., Green, M.J., Myers, K.R., & Smith, S.T. (2015). *Graphic medicine manifesto*. The Pennsylvania State University Press.

DeBenedictis, K. (2022). *Russian "hybrid warfare" and the annexation of Crimea: The modern application of Soviet political warfare*. Bloomsbury.

European Commission. (2022). *Proposal for a council implementing decision establishing the existence of a mass influx of displaced persons from Ukraine within the meaning of Article 5 of Council Directive 2001/55/EC of 20 July 2001, and having the effect of introducing temporary protection.* https://eur-lex.europa.eu/legal-content/EN/TXT/?uri=CELEX%3A52022PC0091

Finley, S. (2008). Arts-based research. In J.G. Knowles & A.L. Cole (eds.), *Handbook of the arts in qualitative research: Perspectives, methodologies, examples, and issues* (pp. 72–82). Sage.

Forde, S.D. (2021). Drawing your way into ethnographic research: Comics and drawing as arts-based methodology. *Qualitative Research in Sport, Exercise and Health, 14*(4), 1–20. https://doi.org/10.1080/2159676X.2021.1974929

Forgey, Q. (2022, February 24). "This is going to take time": Biden defends West's response to Putin's war. *Politico*. https://www.politico.com/news/2022/02/24/zelenskyy-russia-path-of-evil-00011327

Kuttner, P.J., Weaver-Hightower, M.B., & Sousanis, N. (2021). Comics-based research: The affordances of comics for research across disciplines. *Qualitative Research, 21*(2), 195–214. https://doi.org/10.1177/1468794120918845

Kyiv Independent [@KyivIndependent]. (2022, March 1). Zelensky: Launching a rocket at the central square of Kharkiv is an outright, undisguised terror. [Tweet.] Twitter. https://twitter.com/KyivIndependent/status/1498608096859537409

Meer, T., & Müller, A. (2021, July). Making "meanwhile …": Representing queer African youth through spontaneous collaborative graphic autoethnography. *Qualitative Research*. https://doi.org/10.1177/14687941211028801

Needham, C. (2015). Public administration. In M. Bevir & R.A.W. Rhodes (eds.), *Routledge handbook of interpretive political science* (pp. 338–351). Routledge.

Ospina, S.M., & Dodge, J. (2005). It's about time: Catching method up to meaning – the usefulness of narrative inquiry in public administration research. *Public Administration Review, 65*(2): 143–157. https://doi.org/10.1111/j.1540-6210.2005.00440.x

Plokhy, S. (2021). *The gates of Europe: A history of Ukraine* (revised ed.). Basic Books.

Rhodes, R.A.W. (2014). "Genre blurring" and public administration: What can we learn from ethnography? *AJPA: Australian Journal of Public Administration, 73*(3), 317–330. https://doi.org/10.1111/1467-8500.12085

Russia's invasion of Ukraine kills 352 civilians, including 14 children. (2022, February 27). Reuters. https://www.reuters.com/world/europe/russias-invasion-ukraine-kills-352-civilians-including-14-children-2022-02-27/

Sildre, J. (2018). *Kahe heli vahel*. Arvo Pärdi Keskus.

Tondo, L. (2022, March 5). Ukraine: UN says more than 1.3 million have fled since Russian invasion began. *The Guardian*. https://www.theguardian.com/global-development/2022/mar/05/ukraine-un-says-more-than-13-million-have-fled-since-russian-invasion-began

Ukraine war live: As it happened. (2022, March 9). *The Guardian*. https://www.theguardian.com/world/live/2022/mar/09/ukraine-news-russia-war-ceasefire-broken-humanitarian-corridors-kyiv-russian-invasion-live-vladimir-putin-volodymyr-zelenskiy-latest-updates?CMP=share_btn_tw

Vogt, A., Said-Moorhouse, L., Ravindran, J., Wilkinson, P., Yeung, J., Lendon, B., George, S., Wagner, M., Vera, A., & Regan, H. (2022, February 26). February 26, 2022 Russia-Ukraine news. CNN. https://edition.cnn.com/europe/live-news/ukraine-russia-news-02-26-22/h_2ef433d476e597ed0a30111e85a66912

Weber, S. (2008). Visual images in research. In J.G. Knowles & A.L. Cole (eds.), *Handbook of the arts in qualitative research: Perspectives, methodologies, examples, and issues* (pp. 41–54). Sage.

ethno GRAPHIC

Editors: Sherine Hamdy (University of California, Irvine) and Marc Parenteau (cartoonist)

This groundbreaking series realizes ethnographic research in graphic novel form. The series speaks to a growing interest in comics as a powerful narrative medium and to the desire for a more creative and collaborative anthropology that engages the public with contemporary issues. Books in the series are informed by scholarship and combine text and image in ways that are accessible, open-ended, aesthetically rich, and that foster greater cross-cultural understanding.

OTHER BOOKS IN THE SERIES

The King of Bangkok, written by Claudio Sopranzetti, illustrated by Sara Fabbri, adapted by Chiara Natalucci (2021)

Light in Dark Times: The Human Search for Meaning, written by Alisse Waterston, illustrated by Charlotte Corden (2020)

Gringo Love: Stories of Sex Tourism in Brazil, written by Marie-Eve Carrier-Moisan, adapted by William Flynn, illustrated by Débora Santos (2020)

Things that Art: A Graphic Menagerie of Enchanting Curiosity, written and illustrated by Lochlann Jain (2019)

Lissa: A Story about Medical Promise, Friendship, and Revolution, written by Sherine Hamdy and Coleman Nye, illustrated by Sarula Bao and Caroline Brewer, lettering by Marc Parenteau (2017)

CPSIA information can be obtained
at www.ICGtesting.com
Printed in the USA
BVHW020721221222
654795BV00001B/2